Find your
balance

All my best,
nikki

p. 125

The Recipe *for* SUCCESS

The Recipe *for*
SUCCESS

CelebrityPress®
Winter Park, Florida

CONTENTS

CHAPTER 1

STIRRING UP SUCCESS REQUIRES THE RIGHT INGREDIENTS

BY JACK CANFIELD

One of the biggest myths in the world today is that, in order to achieve success, you must be smart enough, educated enough, or rich enough—with the right ideas, connections, and timing—in order to reach your goals and achieve the lifestyle of your dreams. But the reality is that these arbitrary requirements simply aren't needed.

The right ingredients are.

When I first conceived of the book idea that eventually became my bestselling series *Chicken Soup for the Soul*, like many successful businesspeople I was simply responding to interest from my students, audiences and clients. Day after day, as I spoke at business conferences, educator conferences and local civic events, I wove compelling stories of overcoming adversity and achieving goals into my speech to illustrate its points and create an impact. Soon, my listeners began approaching me at the back of the room.

Those stories you told from stage, they would ask, are those in a book somewhere?

When enough people asked over time, I realized that these "feel-good" stories were not just teaching people valuable lessons, they were uplifting people's spirit, too. They were changing them in the moment to someone who was more inspired, thoughtful, kind and forward-thinking.

But these stories were just one ingredient for making *Chicken Soup for the Soul* the monumental success it became. For the next two years, as I and my coauthor Mark Victor Hansen—and my office-manager-turned-business-partner Patty Aubery—collected stories, wrote the book, hired a literary agent and eventually found a publisher (after being turned down 144 times), we had to stir into the mix other ingredients like persistence, belief in ourselves, and listening to our intuition.

Those ingredients eventually cooked up what has become the most published non-fiction book series of all time: over 230 titles and more than 500 million books have been printed in 49 languages. Was it easy? No. Did it take hard work? Yes. But what we honed and refined is a recipe for success that can be replicated in any endeavor that YOU choose to pursue in your own life.

Whether it's changing careers, starting a new charity, winning a major award or growing your own business, these ingredients will help assure your success.

INGREDIENT #1: DECIDE WHAT YOU WANT TO DO, BE AND HAVE

One of the most amazing phenomena you'll ever experience as you pursue success is the unexpected phone call, the windfall financial benefit or the uncanny new acquaintance that brings you exactly what you want or need in order to achieve your loftiest goals—almost as if it were planned.

Perhaps you've worked hard and have "grown" yourself to the point where you're finally ready to receive a benefit which had been waiting in the wings all along. But more probably, as researchers have now come to believe, it may simply be a matter of your subconscious mind focusing on and recognizing opportunity when it arrives.

Whatever the explanation, the reality is that what you want, *wants you.* Your goals, desires and needs are patiently waiting to gravitate toward you, once you decide what you truly want. Of course, the main reason why most people don't get what they want is they haven't decided what those "wants" are. They haven't defined their goals—exactly—in clear and compelling detail. After all, how else can your mind know where to begin looking, seeing and hearing if you don't give it specific and detailed goals to achieve?

Clarify Your Vision and Your Values

There's a very powerful technique for helping you define your goals in vivid and compelling detail. But before using this technique to write down your goals…before defining the compelling life you want for yourself, you first must know what your priorities are. Priorities are "wants" that are personally important to you—not those you believe should be important or those you believe the world expects you to value—but what's truly important to you from the deepest place in your heart.

Once you know your "wants," you must also determine your core values. What kinds of activities and priorities are in alignment with your integrity? Which are outside your acceptable limits?

Think about it. You might "want" all the riches and material wealth that could come from selling illegal drugs, but you might find it very difficult to convince your mind and body of your enthusiasm, especially if breaking the law and contributing to broken lives went against your basic values. In fact, engaging in an activity you don't agree with often causes low self-esteem,

THE RECIPE FOR SUCCESS

depression, despondency, even anger. So be sure that what you want matches your values.

Don't Live Someone Else's Dream

Be certain, too, that what you "want" isn't someone else's version of what you should want.

I once met an anesthesiologist who made $350,000 a year, but whose real dream was to work on cars. He had wanted to be a mechanic, but he knew his mother wouldn't approve. My solution? "Give yourself permission to buy a bunch of cars and then work on them on the weekends," I told him. What the anesthesiologist wanted in his heart didn't match his picture of what he thought he should be.

Unfortunately, the sad reality for most people is they simply aren't honest with themselves. If they were, they would realize their "want to's" are almost always bigger than their "shoulds."

Visualize What You Want

To create a checklist of what you want to be, do and have, use the following exercise. You can either audio-record the instructions yourself, then play them back during the exercise, or you can have a friend read the instructions to you.

Begin by listening to some relaxing music and sitting quietly in a comfortable environment. Then, begin visualizing your ideal life exactly as if you are living it.

1. First, visualize your financial situation. How much money do you have in your savings, how much do you make in income? What is your net worth? How much cash flow do you bring in every month? Next...What does your home look like? Where is it? What color are the walls? Are there paintings hanging in the rooms? What do they look like? Walk through your perfect house visually, using your mind's eye.

14

At this point, don't worry about how you'll get that house. Don't sabotage yourself by saying, *I can't live in Malibu because I don't make enough money.* Once you give your mind's eye the picture, your mind will solve the "not enough money" challenge. Simply be honest with yourself about what you truly want. Continue visualizing your perfect home. Next, visualize what kind of car you are driving.

2. Next, visualize your career. What are you doing in your career? Where are you working? Is it your own business? What kind of clients do you have? What is your compensation like? Is it your own business?

3. Then, focus on your free time, your recreation time. What are you doing with your family and friends in the free time you've created for yourself? What hobbies are you pursuing? What kinds of vacations do you take?

4. Next, visualize your body, your physical health, and your emotional life. Are you free and open, relaxed, perseverant, and in a state of joy all day long? What does that look like for you?

5. Then move on to visualizing your relationships with your family and friends. What is your relationship with your family like? Who are your friends? What is the quality of your relationships with friends? What do those friendships feel like? Are they loving, supportive, and empowering? Could they be better?

6. What about your own personal growth? Do you see yourself going back to school, taking training, seeking therapy for a past hurt or growing spiritually?

7. Move on to the community you live in, the community you've chosen. It's ideal, isn't it? What does it look like? What kinds of community activities take place there? What

about your charitable work? What do you do to help others and make a difference? How often every week do you participate in these activities? Who are you helping?

INGREDIENT #2: FIND MENTORS WHO CAN HELP YOU

Most people tend to ask their friends, neighbors, co-workers and siblings for advice on key issues they may be facing in their life. Too often, they ask the advice of others who have never triumphed over a specific hardship or never succeeded in a specific area of expertise. Perhaps this describes you.

An alternative way to get answers and advice is to find a wing to climb under—or three or four. Surround yourself with advisors, mentors, experts and friends who have succeeded in the specific tasks or skills you need to be good at. Approach them and ask for help.

Of course, while it may seem daunting at first to contact successful people and ask for ongoing advice and assistance, it's easier than you think to enlist the mentorship of those who are far, far above you in the areas you'd like to succeed in.

Similarly, truly successful people even know the great value in asking those who *failed* at a certain activity—who failed, and subsequently triumphed. So don't discount these "former failures" as possible mentors for you.

First, Do Your Homework

One of the key strategies for getting people to say yes is to ask the right person and ask in the right way. In other words, give all the reasons why you are asking them and describe what you'll do with any assistance you're given. It's no different with approaching potential mentors. This means you must do your homework—first, in order to develop your list of possible mentors, but secondly, so you'll know what to ask for when you get them on the phone.

One of the easiest ways to research the names and backgrounds of people who have been successful at your area of interest is to read industry magazines, search the internet, ask trade association Executive Directors, attend trade shows and conventions, call fellow entrepreneurs or approach others who operate in this industry or profession.

Look for mentors who have the kind of well-rounded experience you need to access to tackle your goal. When you start seeing a pattern of the same few people being recommended, you know you've identified your possible mentors.

INGREDIENT #3: DEVELOP HABITS THAT WILL PROPEL YOU TO SUCCESS

Many of our daily activities are simply routine. From the time you get up in the morning until you retire at night, there are hundreds of things you do the same way. These include the way you dress, get ready for the day, read the newspaper, drive to the office, greet people, arrange your desk, set up appointments, work on projects, attend meetings, and so on.

If you've been doing these same activities for years, you have developed a set of firmly-entrenched habits. They involve every area of your life including your work, family, income, health, relationships and many more. The sum total of these habits determines how your life operates. Simply stated, this is your normal behavior.

How Habits Really Work

So, what is a habit? Simply stated, a habit is something you do so often it becomes easy. In other words, it's a behavior that you keep repeating. If you persist at practicing a new behavior, eventually it becomes automatic.

When you're developing a new habit, I recommend that you use a "no exceptions policy." In other words, commit to your new habit every single day. It's what separates the people who are successful from the people who are not successful.

Let's say that maintaining excellent health is high on your list of priorities. If so, then exercising three times a week may be the minimum standard to keep you in shape. A *No Exceptions Policy* means you will maintain this exercise habit no matter what happens, because you value the long-term benefits. People who dabble at change will quit after a few weeks or months. And they usually have a long list of excuses why it didn't work out for them.

If you want to distance yourself from the masses and enjoy a unique lifestyle, understand this: your habits will determine your future. Successful people don't drift to the top. It takes focused action, personal discipline and lots of energy every day to make things happen. The habits you develop from this day forward will ultimately determine how your future works out.

Good or Bad, Habits Always Deliver Results

One of the problems in life is that the results of your bad habits usually don't show up until much later in life.

When you develop a chronic bad habit, life will eventually give you consequences. And you may not like those consequences. But here's what you need to really understand: Life will still give you the consequences. Whether you like it or not isn't the issue. The fact is, if you keep on doing things a certain way, you will always get a predictable result. Negative habits breed negative consequences. Successful habits create positive rewards.

How To Start Changing Your Habits

Developing successful habits takes time. In fact, recent scientific studies put the estimated time at about 60 to 66 days to develop a new habit. But before you change a habit, you need to first check how long you have owned it. If you have been doing something repeatedly for 30 years, you may not be able to let go of it in a few short weeks. Acknowledge the fact that a deeply entrenched habit has long roots. It's like trying to sever a multi-stranded fiber that has molded itself, over time, into a single powerful rope. It's very hard to break. Long-time smokers know how difficult it is to break the nicotine habit. Many never do, despite the overwhelming evidence that proves smoking can significantly shorten your life expectancy.

Another factor about changing habits is the potential for slipping back into your old patterns. This can happen when stress levels rise or an unexpected crisis occurs. The new habit may not be strong enough to resist these circumstances, and more time, energy and effort will be required. To ensure consistency, astronauts use a checklist for every single procedure to ensure the same results every time. You can create a similar fail-safe system. It just takes practice. And it's well worth the effort, as you'll see shortly.

Take Action to Change Your Habits Now

Imagine if you only changed four habits a year. Five years from now you'd have 20 positive new habits. Now, here's the thing— would 20 positive new habits make a difference in your results? Of course! Twenty successful habits can bring you all the money you want or need, wonderful loving relationships, a healthier, more energized physical body, plus all sorts of new opportunities. And what if you created more than four new habits a year? Think of the possibilities!

By systematically improving one behavior at a time, you can dramatically improve your overall lifestyle.

There are two action steps for changing your habits: the first is to make a list of all the habits that keep you unproductive. Block out an hour or more to do this so you can really think through this process. Until you clearly understand what is holding you back, it's difficult to create more productive habits. The most common bad habits include:

- Not returning phone calls on time
- Being late for meetings and appointments
- Not attending to paperwork quickly and efficiently
- Texting during phone calls, meetings or in social settings
- Not following up on overdue receivables
- Talking instead of listening
- Forgetting someone's name 60 seconds or less after being introduced
- Working long days with no exercise or breaks
- Not spending enough time with your children
- Having fast-food meals Monday through Friday
- Making reservations at the last minute
- Procrastinating on everything from filing your taxes to cleaning out your garage

Another way to identify your unproductive behavior is to ask for feedback. Talk to people you respect and admire, who know you well. Ask them what they observe about your bad habits. Look for consistency. If you talk to 10 people and eight of them say you never return phone calls on time, pay attention. Remember this: Your outward behavior is the truth, whereas your inner perception of your behavior is often an illusion.

Creating New Habits That Support Your Success

Once you make a list of your unproductive habits, the second step is to change your bad habits into good ones using this formula:

1. **Clearly identify your bad or unproductive habits.** Think about the future consequences of your bad habits. These may not show up until tomorrow, next week or next month. In fact, the real impact could be years away. So when you examine your own bad habits, consider the long-term implications. Be honest with yourself. Your life may be at stake.

2. **Define one new successful habit at a time to work on.**
Usually just the opposite of your bad habit, you should
decide what you *will do* versus what you won't do. For
example, a smoker might say his or her new successful habit
will be to stop smoking. But what will he actually be doing?
What activities will he engage in? To motivate yourself on
your own habits, think of all the benefits and rewards for
adopting your new successful habit. This helps you create
a clear picture of what this new habit will do for you. The
more vividly you describe the benefits, the more likely you
are to take action.

3. **Create an action plan for the one new habit.** Focus on
three immediate action steps that will help you achieve the
new habit, then put them into practice. For example, if you
work long hours at a desk without breaks or exercise, your
action plan might be to: (1) set your smartphone alarm to
alert you once per hour so you can get up and move around,
(2) identify a park a half-mile away that you can walk to
at lunchtime, and (3) get a cordless phone so you can walk
around during lengthy conference calls. Create your action
plan now. Remember, nothing will change until you do.

THE FINAL INGREDIENT: WHEN YOU TAKE ACTION, GO THE EXTRA MILE

In his timeless classic *Think and Grow Rich*, Napoleon Hill
writes: *The main trouble with so many of us is that we see men
who have "arrived," and we weigh them in the hour of their
triumph without taking the trouble to find out how or why they
arrived.*

The truth is that most of the "overnight" success stories you read
about are really the result of decades of hard work, years of extra
effort and a lifetime of perseverance. These people are often
over-achievers—who simply aren't satisfied with "good enough,"
but who seek out opportunities to deliver more, to provide extra
value, to produce 110% and to do a better job.

They are people who go the extra mile.

Almost by force of habit, successful people simply do more. Not surprisingly, this "do more" habit actually helps create new possibilities in their lives, because they're constantly placed in the way of ever greater opportunity. Imagine what would happen to you if you stayed just 15 minutes after the rest of your fellow employees left for the day...or what you could accomplish if you took charge of some activity that was languishing from lack of manpower. Are there circumstances in your life right now where you could do more, provide better value, over-deliver or improve upon what is asked of you?

Do you have the opportunity—but also the personal initiative—to go the extra mile?

The Big Payoff: Why Would Anyone Want to Go the Extra Mile?

Consider the two most important reasons for going the extra mile:
(1) You experience greater rewards for your efforts, at the same time becoming more valuable to your employers, customers and clients.
(2) You experience a personal transformation, becoming more confident, more self-reliant, more enthusiastic, and more influential with those around you...all traits of successful people.

So, what's the pay-off for you? What can you expect from going the extra mile? Surprisingly, most rewards are unexpected...a surprise promotion, an unusual bonus, a greater area of responsibility, or unusually lucrative revenues for your business. But you have to start in order for the rewards to appear.

About Jack Canfield

Known as America's #1 Success Coach, Jack Canfield is the CEO of the Canfield Training Group in Santa Barbara, CA, which trains and coaches entrepreneurs, corporate leaders, managers, sales professionals and the general public in how to accelerate the achievement of their personal, professional and financial goals.

Jack Canfield is best known as the coauthor of the #1 *New York Times* bestselling *Chicken Soup for the Soul®* book series, which has sold more than 500 million books in 47 languages, including 11 *New York Times* #1 bestsellers. As the CEO of Chicken Soup for the Soul Enterprises he helped grow the *Chicken Soup for the Soul®* brand into a virtual empire of books, children's books, audios, videos, CDs, classroom materials, a syndicated column and a television show, as well as a vigorous program of licensed products that includes everything from clothing and board games to nutraceuticals and a successful line of *Chicken Soup for the Pet Lover's Soul®* cat and dog foods.

His other books include *The Success Principles™: How to Get from Where You Are to Where You Want to Be* (recently revised as the 10th Anniversary Edition), *The Success Principles for Teens, The Aladdin Factor, Dare to Win, Heart at Work, The Power of Focus: How to Hit Your Personal, Financial and Business Goals with Absolute Certainty, You've Got to Read This Book, Tapping into Ultimate Success, Jack Canfield's Key to Living the Law of Attraction,* his recent novel, *The Golden Motorcycle Gang: A Story of Transformation and The 30-Day Sobriety Solution.*

Jack is a dynamic speaker and was recently inducted into the National Speakers Association's Speakers Hall of Fame. He has appeared on more than 1000 radio and television shows including Oprah, Montel, Larry King Live, the Today Show, Fox and Friends, and 2 hour-long PBS Specials devoted exclusively to his work. Jack is also a featured teacher in 12 movies including *The Secret, The Meta-Secret, The Truth, The Keeper of the Keys, Tapping into the Source,* and *The Tapping Solution.* Jack was also honored recently with a documentary that was produced about his life and teachings, *The Soul of Success: The Jack Canfield Story.*

Jack has personally helped hundreds of thousands of people on six different continents become multi-millionaires, business leaders, best-selling authors, leading sales professionals, successful entrepreneurs, and world-class athletes while at the same time creating balanced, fulfilling and healthy lives.

His corporate clients have included Virgin Records, SONY Pictures, Daimler-Chrysler, Federal Express, GE, Johnson & Johnson, Merrill Lynch, Campbell's Soup, Re/Max, The Million Dollar Forum, The Million Dollar Roundtable, The Young Entrepreneurs Organization, The Young Presidents Organization, the Executive Committee, and the World Business Council.

Jack is the founder of the Transformational Leadership Council and a member of Evolutionary Leaders, two groups devoted to helping create a world that works for everyone.

Jack is a graduate of Harvard, earned his M.Ed. from the University of Massachusetts, and has received three honorary doctorates in psychology and public service. He is married, has three children, two step-children and a grandson.

For more information, visit:

- www.JackCanfield.com
- www.CanfieldTraintheTrainer.com

CHAPTER 2

A SUCCESS PLAN FOR PAIN-FREE LIVING
AN ANTIDOTE FOR THE OPIOID CRISIS

BY DR. JOHN ROSA & DR. DAVID SEAMAN

The average savvy individual has high hopes for the future. At age 25 or earlier, many highly-motivated people already have organized plans for achieving success and financial freedom before they are 50 years old. Never in these great plans do people set up goals for developing chronic pain, disease, disability, and addiction to opioids or other medications – such negative considerations do not remotely enter the planning and this is because when we are young, we cannot easily conceptualize our physical health status years into the future and how it will affect our lives.

A problem for many people is that they actually plan to develop chronic aches, pain, and disease, *without knowing it,* by pursuing chronic inflammation. Several unhealthy lifestyle factors robustly promote chronic inflammation, those being inadequate sleep, stress, sedentary living, smoking, excess alcohol consumption, and an unhealthy diet. These many pro-inflammatory lifestyle choices are easy to adopt as a consequence of working long hours and getting wrapped up in all of the responsibilities people take on as they march toward financial success.

Initially, the consequences of a pro-inflammatory lifestyle are minor because a 25-year-old body is young and resilient. However, as time moves on and the pro-inflammatory lifestyles are maintained, by the time people reach 30-40 years old, most people no longer feel young and vital. By 30-40, most people are overweight or obese and chronic inflammation typically commonly manifests as aches and pains. By the time one reaches 50 and older, they have likely been pursuing a pro-inflammatory lifestyle for 30 years or longer. Chronic pain, heart disease, diabetes, depression, and hypertension are the most common manifestations of chronic inflammation in those 50 and older.

No one wants to be financially free by 50 or earlier and not be healthy enough to enjoy it, and even worse, be disabled, suffering with chronic pain, and taking multiple medications, and worse, inadvertently getting addicted to opioids. This chapter will outline a success plan for pain-free living that explains how to easily pursue a robustly healthy physical and mental state that will allow you to fully enjoy the fruits of your labor and give you the best chance to live a disease- and pain-free life.

We are also going to outline key issues related to the current pain crisis, including how pain develops and emerges over time, various pain treatment options, and key issues about the opioid crisis.

A PHILOSOPHY OF LIFE FOR PAIN-FREE LIVING

As we go through life, we go through cycles of injury and healing, and then, we are going to eventually die. People often mistake such a statement to be negative. In fact, the opposite view is true.

Avoiding these realities will lead to the negative health outcomes described earlier. Here is what we mean when this perspective is applied to our financial life. Odds are very strong that you will be poor and exclusively reliant on social security if you do not plan for retirement. You may even have to work into your 70s or 80s for minimum wage to help make ends meet. Clearly, planning for retirement can make our latter years far less financially painful. No one disagrees with this financial view of life, and our suggestion in this chapter is that we should apply this financial thinking to health and wellness.

Just as we hopefully prepare for a successful financial retirement, we need to prepare for inevitable injuries and aging that will occur. If your lifestyle is anti-inflammatory, then you will have the greatest chance to avoid chronic disease expression, effectively bounce back from injuries, and age gracefully without chronic pain. If, on the other hand, you live a pro-inflammatory lifestyle, it is very likely that you will suffer with chronic pain sooner or later to a degree that will surprise you.

FACTS ABOUT YOUR BODY AND MIND

The human body is made of chemicals; our tissues and cells are made of protein, fat, carbohydrates, water, vitamins and minerals. Not surprisingly, body movements, visceral organ function, thoughts, and emotions are all chemical events. The goal should be for these chemical events to be anti-inflammatory, and for this to occur we need sleep, exercise, stress management, proper rest, smoking cessation, moderation of alcohol intake, and an anti-inflammatory diet. This gives us the best chance of living a disease-free and pain-free life.

HOW PAIN EMERGES AND BECOMES CHRONIC

Pain scientists have made it abundantly clear that pain cannot exist without inflammation. In terms of lifestyle, inflammation almost always appears before symptoms manifest. Consider the following scenario.

The human body is made of trillions of cells, which communicate with each other throughout the lifespan by releasing chemicals. The state of this chemical communication can be broadly classified as being pro-inflammatory, non-inflammatory, or anti-inflammatory. In fact, our bodies need to be able to shift among all three states based on the needs of the body.

For example, consider someone who is fortunate to be healthy and robust; this person's body is chemically living in a non-inflammatory state. If this person sprains their ankle, a pro-inflammatory response will generate pain that will require activity modification so the injury can heal. As the injured ankle is rested, anti-inflammatory responses occur that promote healing and bring the person back to their baseline non-inflammatory state.

As we age and adopt the pro-inflammatory lifestyle factors described earlier, the baseline chemical state of the body shifts away from being non-inflammatory to being pro-inflammatory. When this occurs, the same ankle sprain will hurt more, take more time to heal, is more easily re-injured, and can develop chronic pain.

There are gradations in which the human body transforms from a healthy non-inflammatory state into a pro-inflammatory state. The most obvious example of this transformation is the gradual accumulation body fat. We become fat by stressing, not sleeping enough, not exercising, and by eating too many calories. The average American consumes almost 60% of their calories from refined sugar, flour, and oil, in the form of desserts, snacks, sweetened beverages, bread, pastries, pizza, and deep-fried food. Because these calories taste good, the average person tends to overeat them on a daily basis. These calories are pro-inflammatory from two perspectives: they lack anti-inflammatory nutrients and rapidly promote body fat accumulation.

As body fat accumulates, the cell types and chemistry begin to change within the growing fat mass. Body fat, also called adipose tissue, is made up of two cell types, those being fat cells and immune cells. When we are lean and healthy, our fat cells are small and the immune cells are anti-inflammatory. When we become overweight and obese, our fat cells increase in size and the anti-inflammatory immune cells that promote body healing are replaced by pro-inflammatory immune cells that prevent healing. The pro-inflammatory immune cells release pro-inflammatory chemicals that circulate around the body and subtly prevent normal tissue healing.

Body fat accumulation also correlates with pro-inflammatory changes that you will see on a blood test. As body fat rises, so do circulating levels of blood glucose. Circulating lipids also become pro-inflammatory, such that triglycerides and LDL cholesterol levels increase, with an accompanying reduction of HDL cholesterol. Blood pressure also starts to rise, as does a marker of inflammation known as C-reactive protein. Smoking and excess alcohol intake add to the inflammatory burden.

These many pro-inflammatory chemical changes that develop as we age and gain weight are initially without symptoms, so that people are under the illusion that they are still healthy. Unfortunately, the presence of these pro-inflammatory chemical changes slowly promotes cancer, heart disease, Alzheimer's disease, and chronic pain.

At some point, we get injured and in response, local cells release inflammatory chemicals. The problem is that people only consider the injury as causing the pain. People do not realize that their bodies have morphed into a pro-inflammatory and pro-pain state before they were injured. In other words, people live in a low-grade injury/inflammation/pain state of body chemistry, but do not display symptoms to any significant degree until they are actually injured. With injury an acute increase of inflammation is added to the chronic state.

Special pain nerve cells located peripherally in muscles and joints, called nociceptors, are activated by the inflammatory chemistry. The greater the inflammation, the greater the activation of the pain nerve cells, which then stimulate the pain system in the spinal cord. Unfortunately, chronic inflammation causes the peripheral and spinal cord pain system to become overstimulated or hyperexcited, the outcome of which can be severe pain that is debilitating.

The treatment of pain should be two-fold. First, patients should be encouraged to robustly engage in anti-inflammatory lifestyles – get enough sleep, avoid stressors, stay as active as possible (pain permitting), and eat an anti-inflammatory diet, such as The DeFlame Diet. Second, pain patients should be triaged based on the clinical presentation so the most appropriate treatments are delivered. Opiates are not required for the treatment of most painful conditions. This will be outlined in the remaining sections of this chapter.

WHEN PAIN TREATMENT LEADS TO OPIOID ADDICTION, OVERDOSE, AND HOPE

Opioid medications are commonly prescribed for both acute and chronic pain. Patients develop a tolerance to the initial dosage and need more and stronger doses to achieve adequate pain relief. This is when the prescribing physician starts to pull back on prescribing for fear of addiction. Unfortunately such a patient is already addicted, which leads to "doctor shopping" for a prescription, stealing pills from friends and family, and then buying pills on the street. As much as one thinks they will never use a needle, eventually as tolerance elevates and the cost of pills is prohibitive, self-injecting of heroin becomes a cheaper and stronger alternative.

What follows is an all too common scenario. A male patient, who is 29 years of age, seeks further evaluation for his chronic pain of 3 years duration. He is noticeably depressed and emotional in his description of the source of his pain. He was involved in a car accident 3 years prior and was taken to the hospital. He was given a disability note for work and sent home to rest with a 30-day supply of OxyContin, a prescription opioid.

The young man lived with his mother who was already taking the same opioid medication for a chronic pain issue after she was involved in a similar accident 10 years before her son. Neither of them received any treatment for the musculoskeletal trauma other than the medication and as a result they proceeded to refill their opioid prescriptions. Each was eventually labeled as a chronic pain patient and referred for treatment in a pain management facility, which continued to prescribe opioids. As they built up a tolerance to the prescription opioid, they needed more of it to get the same pain relief, and so they turned to street pills and eventually a cheaper version of heroin.

The young man explains that he acquired heroin on the street, for he and his mother, which was laced with carfentanyl, a newer and deadlier synthetic opioid to hit the streets. As a result, they both overdosed and his mom passed away.

After surviving the overdose (and receiving a detox intervention), the son engaged in an Integrative Medicine treatment program that included chiropractic, physical therapy, nutritional therapy, medical message, yoga therapy, mindfulness training, and behavioral medicine for the treatment of pain. Nine months into treatment, the young man was drug free. In our experience, this outcome is the rule rather than the exception. And when patients are treated with such an integrative medicine approach, they can avoid using opioid medications in the first place and never be pushed into a state of addiction, despair, overdose and potentially death.

A total of 80% of heroin users can trace their addiction to a prescription opioid, the majority of which were absolutely unnecessary. Consider the fact that the United States represents a mere 5% of the world's population and yet we consume over 90% of the world's opioid supply. There are only two explanations for this situation. First, only Americans suffer from painful injuries and need opioids, which is not true. Second, we have been over-prescribed opioids in America for the last several decades. Obviously, the latter is true.

CURRENT OPIOID STATISTICS

Current statistics are eye opening. According to many sources (White House, CDC, Department of Justice, Drug Enforcement Agency, Homeland Security, Border Patrol and state police), the scale of the opioid crisis is actually underreported and getting worse. 2017 data reveals the following daily opioid events:

- 650,000 prescriptions for opioids
- 4,000 start non-medical use
- 600 start heroin use
- 3,300 opioid-related ER visits
- 58 babies born addicted
- 120 die of overdose

In our opinion, the current opioid crisis requires a three-tiered approach: Awareness, Prevention, and Non-opioid treatments. Each will be discussed in more detail in the following paragraphs.

1. Awareness of the opioid crisis

Most people were aware that opioid drugs are addictive before the emergence of the current opioid crisis. However, most are not aware of how aggressively addictive they actually are. For example, taking an opioid for just one day leads to a 6% risk of use one year later. If opioids are taken for 8 days, this leads to a 13.5% risk of use one year later and a 30-day prescription carries a 30% risk. Any patient prescribed an opioid medication should be aware of this risk. What this risk information also tells us is that the most abusive and unsuspecting cause of the opioid problem is actually following a physician's prescribing orders.

When someone is seen by a physician for any pain-related condition, it was historically, and today still remains a common practice to prescribe an opioid for a painful condition. This for many is the beginning of the end. The general public needs to be aware that opioids, in all their forms, are highly addictive, no matter if they are prescribed by a physician or acquired from the street.

Lastly, the general public needs to understand that the opioid crisis is the outcome of an extremely lucrative business model for opioid manufacturers. Consider that just one company, Purdue Pharma, the manufacturer of OxyContin, has generated some $35 billion in revenue. In the United States, the drug companies that manufacture opioids donate eight times more money to Congress than the gun lobby.

2. Opioid crisis prevention

A multi-tiered approach to prevention is our recommendation. The best defense against opioid addiction is to be a health advocate for yourself and family members and ask for alternatives to opioid medications when prescribed. In this regard, we recommend that pain education in medical school be updated to be consistent with the current evidence regarding integrative medicine.

Surprisingly, pain education is very weak in medical school. The outcome is that physicians are not trained to manage pain patients properly, as witnessed by the extremely liberal prescribing patterns of opioid medications. Here is what patients are almost never told about their pain when they see a medical doctor in private practice, hospital, or urgent care center:

- Patients are never told how pain emerges and becomes chronic (as described earlier in this chapter).
- Patients are never told how a pro-inflammatory lifestyle promotes chronic pain expression (as described earlier in this chapter).
- Patients are never told that multiple non-drug and non-surgery treatments can be extremely effective treatments for pain (as described earlier in this chapter).

When we are able to engage pain patients before they are prescribed opioids, and treat these patients with medicine, chiropractic, physical therapy, yoga therapy, mindfulness and nutritional therapy, there has been a substantial reduction in opioid prescriptions in our clinics. For example, we placed our team directly into a primary care physicians office seeing over 100 patients per day and reduced their opioid prescriptions by 70%. In other words, when the proper integrative medicine treatment program is utilized to reduce pain, it functions as a strong preventive measure against opioid use and addiction.

3. Integrative medicine approach to pain treatment

Previously in this chapter, we outlined lifestyle factors to help reduce pain expression. It is the job of the individual to make sure that he/she is making healthy and anti-inflammatory lifestyle choices. Some people are very successful at sticking to an anti-inflammatory lifestyle, while others find it useful to engage physicians, trainers, or health coaches to keep them on track. Whatever works for you is what you should do.

We also listed the key non-pharmacological and non-surgical treatments that are useful in treating pain. It is the job of the integrative medical team to make sure that effective treatments are selected for the individual needs of the patient. The key is to find a physician group that delivers integrative medicine under the same roof, which helps to guarantee that a patient will get the care they need.

Another dimension of care needs to be considered when dealing with pain patients that are already addicted to opioid drugs. This involves a focused commitment by the addicted patient, a family-friend support system, and finding the appropriate physicians to help manage the process of recovery. There are several recovery domains that need to be address and incorporated into one's lifestyle for the remainder of their life.

Drug detoxification:
- Look for a medical or hospital drug detoxification program
- Post detoxification treatments for physical and mental health
- Investigate medically-assisted treatments (methadone, naltrexone, buprenorphine)

Environment:
- Live in a drug-free environment
- Seek friends and family that will support recovery

Personal mental emotion factors:
- Find a community to be part of, such as faith-based groups
- Be of service to others and your community
- Finish your education
- Get and hold a good job
- Engage in goal planning for the future

Personal health practices:
- Follow The DeFlame Diet

- Take nutritional supplements
- Exercise regularly

You should recognize that the title and content of these four domains could be slightly modified, and then serve as a plan for achieving any goal, such as weight loss, fitness, relationship success, a successful retirement, and business success.

About Dr. John Rosa

Dr. John P. Rosa owns and supervises Accessible Beltway Clinics, which is comprised of 16 clinics in Maryland and Virginia, combining medicine, chiropractic, physical therapy, acupuncture and behavioral medicine to give a comprehensive multidisciplinary approach to pain syndromes and musculoskeletal disorders.

He is active in sports medicine with consulting/treating college, professional and Olympic athletes. Dr. Rosa is the creator of 24/7 **RnR** (**R**elief and **R**ecovery) – an FDA approved analgesic cream. He is also the founder of Accessible Wellness Solutions – an onsite corporate wellness program offering consulting, lectures and clinic management.

-- *Leader in Chiropractic*
- Trustee of New York Chiropractic College for over 15 years and serving final 3-year term as Chairman of the Board.

-- *Integrative Medicine Specialist:*
- Board service to Maryland University of Integrative Health
- Consultant on Integrative Medicine to hospital cancer center
- Reduced opioid prescriptions by 70% by integrating Chiropractic, physical therapy and behavioral medicine in a primary care setting
- Expert/Speaker - educating primary care, urgent care and hospital medical staff on the Integrative Medicine approach to treating pain patients

-- *Opioid Crisis Expert:*
- White House Surrogate/Consultant
- Law Enforcement Consultant (Homeland Security, CBP, DOJ, DEA and Postal)
- State and National Consultant to Opioid Task Forces
- Corporate and professional organization consultant
- Currently forming the Opioid Abuse Prevention Institute

-- *Community Leadership:*
- Board member of the National Italian-American Foundation
- Volunteer at Crossroads Freedom Center - a residential facility in Maryland to help overcome addiction

If you would like to learn more about the Opioid Crisis as it relates to awareness, prevention and treatment or schedule a corporate or organization seminar contact us at: DrJohnRosa.com. Here you will learn how to connect you, your company or organization with the leading experts on the crisis and how to help your community stay safe.

- Contact: DrJohnRosa.com

About Dr. David Seaman

Dr. David Seaman has been writing about chronic inflammation for 25 years. He wrote the first published scientific article about how diet can induce inflammation and promote pain. His articles about pain, inflammation, diet, and obesity have been referenced by researchers at the Centers for Disease Control (CDC), Harvard Medical School and many other universities in the United States, as well as universities in Canada, Brazil, Europe, Middle East, India, Australia, Russia, and other Asian countries.

In 2016, Dr. Seaman wrote a book for the general public entitled, The DeFlame Diet. The focus of this book is how to measure and reduce chronic inflammation through dietary means. It is the most detailed book on this topic that is written for the general public. If you want a simple approach to diet, the DeFlame approach is the way to go.

In 2018, he published *Weight Loss Secrets You Need To Know*, which is available as a *free* Kindle book for Prime members and otherwise for .99 cents, which is the lowest Kindle allows. This new book outlines the many societal, sensory, emotional, physiological, and primordial drives that promote weight gain and obesity. Without understanding the power of these non-food factors related to obesity, it is virtually impossible to manage weight properly in the long term. Obesity is a health menace and this book offers a strategy for maintaining proper weight for a lifetime.

- www.DeFlame.com
- YouTube channel: DeFlame Nutrition
- Facebook: DeFlame Nutrition

CHAPTER 3

INSPIRED SUCCESS: ALIGNED FROM WITHIN, MANIFESTED OUTSIDE THE BOX, TRANSFORMATIVE BY DESIGN

BY TERI P. COX, PRESIDENT, COX COMMUNICATIONS PARTNERS, LLC

I'll never forget the first time I encountered "success" defined in a way that touched me deeply. It made an indelible impact.

Raised in my middle class neighborhood in Pittsburgh, PA, I'd just graduated from 8th grade. Gearing up for high school in an accelerated program, I was excited about the future. One graduation gift from my beloved parents, now a treasured keepsake, was a porcelain coffee mug with a rainbow on it, inscribed with this inspiring quote from Emerson:

Success

"To laugh often and much; to win the respect of intelligent people and the affection of children; to earn the appreciation of honest critics and endure the betrayal of false friends; to appreciate beauty; to find the best in others; to leave the world a bit better, whether by a healthy child, a garden patch or a redeemed social condition; to know even one life has breathed easier because you have lived. That is to have succeeded."

On reading it, I knew immediately I wanted that for my life! I wanted to achieve that kind of impact – make the world better; make a difference for many lives, not just one. It fit perfectly with my parents' values, my upbringing. It fit my nature – warm, caring and compassionate; someone always concerned about others, who connects from the heart. My parents' gift was meant to influence my future, and it did.

Improving the world by making a difference for others became my passion, my purpose. I'm grateful to have found many ways for it to manifest over the years, with notable success and personal fulfillment. My quality of life and spirituality were transformed in the process. It still drives me forward today.

Given that, as I reflect on my amazing life journey as a change agent over 40+ years, I owe much of my success to three additional factors that set me ahead early on as a student, then in my career and life.

The first is that I was blessed with a creative and analytical mind, disciplined with keen memory, attention for details and commitment to high performance and quality standards. Those mental strengths helped me succeed scholastically and professionally. I've always pushed myself to do better.

For example, while a student, I did well in my courses, except Physical Ed. I wasn't athletic. So, I took four dance courses – determined to master them all. I still love dancing today!

I've learned to always give my best to my studies, the positions I've held, the projects and leadership roles I take on and in my relationships.

Those strengths also helped me appreciate and learn about the power of words. I came to realize that I LOVE writing, honed my talents as a storyteller, wordsmith and editor, then later as a strategist and communicator in a larger sense.

The second is that I've learned to think strategically to visualize "big picture" ideas and goals and tactically to determine steps and resources needed to make them happen. That's a plus for any project manager, executive or entrepreneur. Most people are strong in one or the other, but not both.

I'm a team player, but independent thinker about most things. Using my creative side, I've learned to consider fresh ideas, while my analytical side asks questions, thinks through practical solutions. Combining both thought processes, I don't accept the status quo when improvement or change makes good sense.

It's natural for me to think *outside the box* to find better options, innovative ways for meeting challenges, problems or needs and seeking new opportunities.

The third factor comes into play whenever I seek clarity, need to dig deeper, tackle a critical question or navigate through a challenge while trying to achieve a goal. That's when I've learned to access and trust my intuition.

In stillness, I close my eyes, go inward and listen for my inner voice. Through contemplation and meditation, I focus on questions and ask my Divine Power within to guide me to the right answers. It takes time, but I've learned it's worth the wait. I KNOW in my heart when it feels right. Then, I take action with clarity and confidence.

As I've mentored others about much of this over the years, I've enjoyed when their eyes lit up and their minds opened up to new ways of thinking, and a sense of fresh possibilities.

START WITH WHAT YOU KNOW

No matter where you are on the journey toward manifesting greater success in your life and career, it's important to know your essential strengths, passions, preferences and gifts.

The more you understand about yourself, the more you can focus on what really matters, what you love doing and brings joy, what fits your personality and values, differentiates you from others. The Passion Test, by Janet Bray Attwood and Chris Attwood, is a great tool for finding your passion and purpose. When that's clear, you're on the right path.

STRETCH YOUR THINKING *OUTSIDE THE BOX* AND COMMIT TO EXCELLENCE

As you analyze how to align your passion with your strengths to fulfill unmet needs or provide a better way, don't limit yourself – celebrate your uniqueness, be creative, raise your standards!

It's important to look beyond the ordinary, and what most others and competitors are doing. Conduct research to identify what might be a totally different, enhanced or superior approach to your business. Push beyond what's comfortable. Thinking strategically and acting *outside the box* takes vision and courage, but adds value by stimulating innovation. You can learn more about strategic thinking at: www.morebusiness.com or through books and videos by Harvard professor, Michael Porter.

That kind of thinking can help you identify more meaningful and lucrative ways to provide service and value to others – whether to an employer, your clients, customers, patients or your audience – whatever group or constituents your passion guides you to serve. When manifested, those ideas can separate you from the pack, with less competition and more self-designed opportunity for greater success, especially when you deliver beyond expectations.

ACCESS THE POWER OF YOUR INTUITIVE WISDOM

As you're strategizing your big goals and dreams for the future, "unplug" from daily distractions. Allow time for stillness and deep breathing. Learn meditation techniques for connecting with your intuition. Both Jack Canfield and Deepak Chopra provide great guidance and resources about meditation.

As you go inward, visualize your goals and dreams as if they were already materializing. Ask your inner wisdom for guidance on steps to achieve them, or questions you have about how to proceed. When inspiration comes, listen and take notes. Follow through with action. Over time, the way will become more clear.

INTEGRATING THESE FACTORS BRINGS GREATER SUCCESS

Allow your intuition to help you integrate your passion with your essential strengths to accelerate progress. Once you put it all together, you'll gain more confidence, a deeper understanding of all you bring to the table. The Universe will respond by opening new doors for expanding your horizons. You'll connect with like-minded people for potential collaboration, partnerships and more. Over time, you'll broaden your skillset, realize new strengths you didn't know you had.

Keep your mind open to new possibilities! Your professional and personal life experience will evolve exponentially from there.

Here are some examples:

1. I learned to integrate my purpose with my strengths and started on my intuitive path while I was at the University of Pittsburgh in the 1970's.

   I started as an English major. After my first term, I knew that wasn't enough. I also took journalism and speech courses, while considering a career in broadcasting. But, Pitt didn't have a full Communications program at that time. I enjoyed Pitt, with no desire to change schools. Thinking it through, I came up with a novel idea back then – a self-designed major in Communications, cross-registering for courses in media, film editing and broadcasting at Carnegie Mellon University near Pitt campus to complete my major. Two professors thought it was a great idea and became my faculty sponsors. I learned how to navigate and set the system in place at both universities to make it happen.

   That was my first successful experience combining analytical, creative, strategic and tactical outside-the-box thinking with my intuition to find a better way. It became my new standard.

2. A second experience happened during my junior year, at my work-study job at the University Women's Center.

   Decades before computers and search engines, as administrative assistant at the Center, I fielded calls from women needing help with personal crises, health issues, dangers from abuse, rape, housing and child care needs, legal problems and more.

   I created an intake form and gathered information from each caller. Then, I conducted phone outreach to social service, medical, legal, educational, government and religious organizations for resources to meet each caller's needs.

Over six months, I tracked calls, documented repeat-call categories, demographics and caller locations. It was clear that women throughout the area needed help with a wide range of issues and problems. I did intuitive brainstorming about the best way to address this need. It came to me as I visualized a book – Pittsburgh needed a women's resource directory! I was determined to make it happen.

I minored in Women's Studies, so I met with that program's Chair, the Executive Director of the Women's Center and Dean of the College of Arts and Sciences to discuss my idea. All enthusiastically supported it. I received a grant as project coordinator of a three-term independent study.

I selected topics for sections, developed a list of resources, templates for entries, and recruited and supervised a team of students who worked with me to collect comprehensive information.

Then, I graduated, with the first BA degree in Communications and Speech from the University of Pittsburgh.

After graduation, I received another grant, was assigned a full-time typist and hired by the University to edit and produce, *HELP YOURSELF: A Women's (People's) Resource Directory for Pittsburgh*, published in 1975. Sold in area book stores, the directory became a bestseller and helped thousands of women.

I handled the PR and media interviews. Pitt received local, regional and national publicity. The visibility launched my career!

I received several job offers. Following my passion, I became PR director of the local Mental Health Association. While there, I gained experience in media relations and organizing conferences. What I learned about advocacy, creating win-win partnerships between non-profit organizations and companies and effective non-profit board leadership helped position me, providing a solid foundation for building my reputation and every career success I've had since then.

Adding those skills to my professional repertoire manifested many more opportunities aligned with my passion and strengths and has taken my career and life to new levels for decades. It's still happening.

After the women's directory project, I also was hired as producer/ host of "Impact," a radio talk show on two local stations. My guests included authors, celebrities, officials from government and local organizations, and corporate spokespeople.

My life-changing interview was with a spokesman from an oil corporation headquartered in Pittsburgh. He was on to discuss the Arab oil embargo. We had an informative interview. Afterwards, I recruited him to chair my media committee at the Mental Health Association. He also served on our board of directors. Together, we worked on United Way campaigns with the great Steelers and Pirates teams of that decade, all active supporters. He became my mentor and trusted friend.

In the early 1980's, Bill Cox became my beloved husband and life partner. We shared a wonderful life together, successful on all fronts for decades until he lost his cancer battle. The life I knew changed forever. With time spent in silence and meditation, help from my intuition and other resources, my healing began. I learned important life lessons and was spiritually transformed. I've planned to share those lessons to help others. Now, I'm focused on my new life chapter. And, I'm still dancing!

Change is inevitable. No matter your level of success, you'll have ups and downs, wins and losses. How you respond makes all the difference. I've learned that what doesn't kill you, transforms you – NEVER give up!

God's two greatest gifts to us are this amazing journey called LIFE and a powerful, resilient human spirit that can transcend beyond any challenge or darkness, shine brightly again and again and soar to new heights.

Stay positive! Keep dreaming. Make a difference – the world needs your passion and gifts. Here's to your success!

About Teri

With passion, integrity and creativity, Teri P. Cox has dedicated her life and career to challenging the status quo, finding innovative solutions, and advocating for positive change. Teri has provided leadership and expertise to inform marketers and government officials, empower professional women and cancer patients and survivors, train advocacy volunteers and support caregivers across the country. As a change agent, Teri's made a difference for millions.

For over 40 years, Teri has held positions or served as consultant with major pharmaceutical companies and PR agencies, trade associations, educational institutions and non-profit organizations. Combining strengths in market research, project management, PR, writing and editing with her healthcare savvy, Teri launched her award-winning firm, Cox Communications Partners, LLC in 1992. Teri elevates her clients above the fray by positioning them strategically and helping them build win-win partnerships with stakeholders linked to their mission and goals. She's directed successful national advocacy and healthcare policy projects, patient education and disease-awareness campaigns, healthcare marketing and corporate programs.

For decades, Teri also was caregiver for her parents who had Alzheimer's and heart disease, then her husband before he lost his cancer battle. Understanding the burden of family caregivers, Teri recruited an advisory council of organizations involved in aging, caregiving and healthcare – including AARP, National Council on the Aging, Alzheimer's Association, and Interfaith Caregivers Alliance. As project manager/editor for her client company sponsor, Teri partnered with them to create *"CARING TO HELP OTHERS,"* a comprehensive program to help organizations train volunteers assisting caregivers of chronically-ill older adults. This award-winning program has helped over 13,000 community organizations across the U.S.

Teri has held board leadership positions with the Healthcare Business-women's Association, a professional organization committed to furthering the advancement and impact of women in healthcare worldwide, and the American Cancer Society (ACS), serving New York and New Jersey. She received the St. George Medal, the top national honor awarded to ACS volunteers.

Currently, Teri is a board member of Grounds For Sculpture, a renowned sculpture park, museum and arboretum in Hamilton, NJ, founded by artist and philanthropist Seward Johnson.

Teri has an MBA in Marketing from New York University/Stern School of Business and a BA in Communications and Speech from the University of Pittsburgh. At Pitt, Teri led the independent study, then became editor of *HELP YOURSELF: A Women's (People's) Resource Directory for Pittsburgh*, published by the University of Pittsburgh, and a consultant for the second, expanded edition. She also produced and hosted *Impact*, a radio talk show on local stations.

Teri has been featured in *Redbook* magazine, *Pharmaceutical Executive*, *PR News* Corporate Social Responsibility Guidebook, and *PharmaVOICE: The Forum for the Industry Executive*, for which she was named one of the *PharmaVOICE* 100 most inspiring people in the life sciences industry. Inspired by her transformation after serious life changes, Teri is writing her memoir, *MY PATH TO BUTTERFLY: Transformative Lessons About Courage and Resilience from a Self-Designed Life*. As a speaker, Teri is dedicated to helping others navigate through major challenges, loss and change by sharing her inspiring message, compelling *Butterfly Legacy* and hopeful advice.

You can connect with Teri at:

- tcox@coxcommpartners.com
- www.linkedin.com/teripcoxmba

CHAPTER 4

WHICH LETTER DO YOU WANT TO WRITE?

BY RAFAEL NACIF

Having so-called success early in life didn´t come without a price. I was only 32 when I sold my company. I was being recognized as a young successful entrepreneur, had a seven-figure bank account, traveled all over the world, slept at the best hotels, dove with sharks in Hawaii and climbed snowed peaks in the Swiss Alps. I was at the top of the world, so I thought.

My name is Rafael Nacif and I have a hobby. Every year I do at least one long trip in some exotic country. By bicycle. I´ve biked the Atlas Mountains in Morocco, peddled across rice fields in south Vietnam, played soccer with kids in rural Cambodia, and biked along the clear waters of Thailand, just to name a few. None the less, the trip that touched me most profoundly was back at home in beautiful Portugal.

In the midst of this endless search for success, little by little, I let some important areas of life slip away.

a. Health

I remember stepping on the scale and the doctor telling me. Look, if you love your children, you´d better start looking after your health or you will not see them growing up. I had high cholesterol, was overweight and had cardiac arrhythmia. In brief, not a great scenario for a young pal.

b. Time

My daughter Sophia was born premature after my wife Patricia had a condition at her birth called pre-eclampsia. I risked leaving the hospital without both mother and daughter. Not what I´ve imagined. Nevertheless, I was absent. Today I feel ashamed of not having personal memories of the first year of Sophia's life.

c. Family

Having a deep pocket at an early age left me thinking I could do it all. . .be in every project. . .buy every building, and consequently buy friends and happiness. I wanted to embrace the world, I had investments on three continents but only had the same 24 hours in a day as everyone else. I took some wrong turns and I remember coming home one day after making many mistakes, and thinking: If this investment does not pick up, I won´t have the money to pay my mortgage. I looked at my two daughters and my wife and cried.

d. Work

For two years, all I did was travel and work. A lot of my physical body was at home but my mind was away, onto some new and exciting project. My gold flight business card was always in use. When the flight attendants faces started to be familiar, I knew there was something wrong. Investment groups invited me to their private meetings in London. The future looked bright. But not every side of it.

e. Marriage

My wife was suffering. My daughters didn´t have their father with them. I had money but I couldn´t buy peace. I had a big house, but love was leaving through the front door. I had it all, but missed the essentials.

After this unreachable search for success, I soon found out that I was just a person with money but no purpose.

It was a normal Thursday morning. I traveled to the beautiful city of Porto in the north of Portugal for another meeting where we were presented with a potential start up, looking for seed money to get their idea off the ground. I took my bike with me, and after a delicious cod with olive oil for lunch, I took my bike as I had previously planned, and I decided to ride my bike back home, some 215 miles away.

By the end of the second day, just arriving on the world-famous coastal town of Nazaré, known for its giant waves, it started to rain. I had ridden more then 60 miles on that day and I have to confess I was tired. As I was riding along the coast it started to rain and the beautiful sun gave place to some grey sky and heavy clouds.

For some strange reason, I started to cry, and as I cried, a deep feeling of death took me by storm. Deep inside of me, I had a question to which I couldn´t find an answer. What if I had a terminal illness that I knew I was going to die in three months from now? That question resonated in every cell of my body and I couldn´t hold the tears mixing now with the rain that was pouring from the sky.

I stopped the bike and as I looked into the ocean to find an answer, I´ve decided to write two letters to my daughters. These letters, as I later wrote in my hotel room, expressed my deepest and sincere feelings about the greatness of our lives.

Letter #1:

Dear Anna and Sophia,

Daddy was a very successful man. Daddy won't be here much longer, but I would like to leave you a message from my heart. As you know, Daddy had the illusion of being a very important person.

Success for me meant always saying YES to everyone, to every project and to everything. I didn't have time to play peak-a-boo or run in the park. I wasn't present at your musical at school nor did I take you to swim classes, because I had a lot of success.

I was too busy. Busy being successful. Going after things to accumulate even more things to be more successful. All I wanted were things. Daddy didn't have time for you.

As Daddy goes far away, the love, compassion, teachings and feelings, that I won't leave you because I've never had the time. I'll leave you with companies, buildings and a lot of things. Daddy was a very successful man.

Letter #2:

Dear Anna and Sophia,

Daddy was a very successful man.

I remember the first time you've smiled to me, crawled on the floor, stood up alone and said "Papa." I felt so privileged to be there at these moments. I felt very successful.

I remember hiking with you in Switzerland, on a very high mountain, and when we arrived at the peak we looked down. We opened our arms together and felt we were the kings and queens of the world.

We arrived at Geneva airport with our few pieces of luggage and you. Still little babies. Starting life in a new country. Knowing no one. Tough times. Meaningful times. Memories forever.

The first time we've traveled alone was magical. We created true connection. We played at the beach. We played on the sand. We lived life to its fullest.

Daddy will leave you now, but our memories together will be eternal. No money, no things, nothing can replace the beautiful moments we've spent together. We lived a truly happy life. I was a very successful man.

As I've wrote these letters, I've found out that, yes, I wanted to be successful, and yes, I wanted to have a great life. The only problem is that I had the wrong recipe for it. I soon developed my own recipe for success. The one that I now know and share with you. When I reach my last days of life, I won't regret pursuing it.

And here is my recipe for success:

1. Invest in the people you love

Working as a startup investor, I know that for the startup company to thrive, I need to invest my money, my time and my knowledge, otherwise it will not succeed. It is not much different with our families and friends, with the people we care for most in our lives. For our relationships to shine, I need to put in real effort, I need to give them quality time, and yes, I also need to spend money. No other investment will bring as high returns. Seeing my two children grow up and being with them in the process is priceless. Going out with friends to a good restaurant or seeing a sunset with my wife brings us joy. Success is much better lived with the people you love. Invest in your family. Invest in your friends.

2. Give more

Greatness is not measured by how much you have but by how much you give. Giving is truly the essence of life. My business partner is truly a giver. He has a good heart and it is always in search of giving something to someone. He does not hide his contacts or his secrets. He gives his time and he invest his money in people. His life is abundant in every aspect: family, socially and financially. He is a giver. Understand that the more you give, the more you will receive. That is true for love, time, knowledge and money. This is one of the laws of the universe. Practice the art of giving with no strings attached and open your arms for a life of abundance.

3. Have less

Never in the history of modern civilization have we had so much stuff. We have larger houses but smaller dwellings, we have fast internet but are unable to connect to each other. We own more t-shirts, more pants, more telephones, we just have more. Understand that. The best things in life are not things. When I´ve decided to give 70% of all my clothes away, and keep only the ones I truly liked, I felt lighter. All my choices pleased me. I stopped comparing myself to others. I could be me again, and I missed me. Have less, be more.

4. Concentrate on the essentials

What is important to you? At one point in my life, everything was important. I was growing tiny little particles every day in every direction. I was achieving nothing. When you concentrate on the essentials, you don´t go everywhere, you don´t go with everyone, you learn to say more 'No´s' and less 'Yeses'. You create real value, you live better, you have more time. You achieve meaningful success. Knowing what is essential to you is knowing your true essence. What is truly important to you? It does not matter what speed you go. It matters what direction you take.

5. Don´t give up on your dreams

Clarity is essential, persistence is powerful. Stop worrying what others will think of you. Only you know. Don't do it because of others, do it for you, do it because of you. You only have one life, make it count. Live truly, live fully. You don´t have to conquer the world, but conquer yourself, conquer your dreams. If you have to regret something, at least regret not achieving it, but don´t regret not trying it. Don´t follow your head, follow your heart, and promise, don´t give up on your dreams!

It does not matter if society thinks you're are successful if you don't feel success within you. If you can´t wake up every day, look at the mirror and admire the person on the other side of it, then your success is not sustainable, and you are not being true to yourself.

Here are some of the people I´ve come across in life who are very successful:

-- After suffering a heart attack at the age of 41, Fernanda abandoned her career as a PR person for a multinational to dedicate herself to her family. She now lives with just a small portion of the income she would have received before. She spends a lot of time with her son and friends. She has never been happier in life.

-- Cesar was on top of his game as a bank consultant. One day he mixed in his life with Marcos, a street child in Brazil. Eight years later, he and his wife have a project that teaches sports to street kids. They´ve helped hundreds of kids to have a better future. He is a very successful man.

-- Katarina decided to sell everything and travel the world. She works as a freelancer in graphic design. She makes 25,000 USD a year. She is living the life of her dreams.

-- Sergio is 65. He drives an Uber in the streets of Lisbon. He loves to tell and listen to stories from people all around the world. Sergio is very excited with the book he is writing, "Stories from an Uber driver". Sergio found meaning in his life.

After living in Brazil, United States, Canada and Switzerland, I now live in a small town in the west coast of Portugal. I am a business owner, an investor and a speaker. My true treasures are the good people who surround me. Every day I say 'no' to good projects. Every day I say 'yes' to what is truly important to me. Every day I choose to be successful.

You can change your reality. You have your recipe for success. Follow it. Don´t procrastinate your life away. Invest in the people you love, give more, have less, concentrate on the essentials and don´t give up on your dreams.

Every day you and I, we write a portion of our letter. One day, we will hand it out. I know which letter I want to write.

Which one are you going to write?

About Rafael

Serial Entrepreneur, keynote speaker, best-selling author, coach, but more important, Rafael Nacif is the father of Anna and Sophia, married to Patricia, and together they have four dogs and a cat.

Since the age of 32, Rafael has helped hundreds of entrepreneurs see the unseen, believe the impossible, follow their deepest dreams and most importantly, be true to themselves.

Originally from Brazil, Rafael left home at the age of 19 to explore the world. He has lived in the beautiful islands of Hawaii, moving later to friendly Montreal, passing a year in Switzerland, only to finally establish himself with his family in the coastal town of Cascais, Portugal.

Rafael is a partner of the Holding Brave Generation, and together with his partner, Tim Vieira (Shark Tank Portugal), they have invested in over 50 companies from a vast range of sectors. Some of these companies include Portal da Queixa, one of the most visited sites in the country for business. Luzboa, a company that provides electrical energy for households in Portugal. Link to Leaders – the leading webportal for articles, information about entrepreneurship. Link to Leaders's goal is to help young entrepreneurs meet potential investors.

His company, Brave Generation, has invested in a cinema studio, and together with young and talented producers, they have produced the movie *Carga*, a movie about Human Trafficking to raise world awareness of this rising problem. Since life is not only work but also fun, Rafael has a wine company called, One More Glass. The company produces four varieties of wines; of these, *Live, Laugh Love* is the most well-known.

Other companies in construction, real estate, hotel and agricultural sectors comprise the rest of the portfolio of Brave Generation.

Rafael is passionate about human development. At one point, he has promised himself he would use his life to change the world and leave a legacy for his daughters, touching and being a light to the people around him. That is his mission. Rafael travels the world with a message – a message of hope, dreams and greatness.

Together with his wife Patricia, they have founded Anna and Sophia's Foundation, to help the underprivileged have access to education, better nutrition and build better communities. Their foundation has helped children in Brazil, Mozambique, Congo, Nepal and Portugal. Rafael believes that the secret of life is giving.

Rafael has created the largest Human Development conference in Portugal, called *Desperta* (Wake Up). This three-day event aims to show people powerful techniques to reach their true potential and to dedicate their lives to what is most important to them. He has also created the tour "Meu Propósito Muda o Mundo", (My mission changes the world), a four-hour seminar dedicated to raise funds for local humanitarian organizations. Rafael and his amazing team of passionate people have touched thousands of lives around the country.

To know more about Rafael and his work, please visit:
- www.rafaelnacif.com

CHAPTER 5

THE NASCAR RULE... AND HOW YOU CAN USE IT TO GROW YOUR BUSINESS!

BY JW DICKS & NICK NANTON

If I had asked people what they wanted, they would have said, 'faster horses.'
~ Henry Ford

The winner ain't the one with the fastest car; it's the one who refuses to lose.
~ Dale Earnhardt

You don't earn loyalty in a day. You earn loyalty day-by-day.
~ Jeffrey Gitomer

In 1948, a local Daytona Beach gas station owner named "Big" Bill France started a new American sport based on a history of illegal bootlegging. The *National Association for Stock Car Auto Racing*, or more commonly known as NASCAR, had its early roots in the mobile transportation of moonshine. During Prohibition, drivers would modify stock cars to increase their speed and storage capacity for hauling the liquor, while outrunning the law.

In the years that followed the end of Prohibition, Bill France saw an opportunity to monetize the South's need for speed. Excitement grew as the dangerous competition fueled the global attention from a string of world land speed records already set in the area. As France began organizing a series of races to test the fastest cars and best drivers, NASCAR gained traction and picked up momentum.

FROM BOOTLEGGING TO GLOBAL BRAND

From its beginning NASCAR and advertising have gone hand-in-hand. Initially, the first sponsors where made up of local businesses. But as time progressed, other larger alcohol, tobacco, and automotive companies joined in. What started out as a bunch of former bootlegging car drivers, known as "shine runners" in and around the Appalachian region of the United States, has since grown into a global brand with developmental projects in Mexico, Canada and Europe. Today, NASCAR is home to top sponsors like Monster Energy, Ford and VISA. The 2017 Daytona 500, the company's flagship race, had a reported brand valuation of $140 million dollars alone.

But for small businesses, services providers and sales professionals that come to the Dicks + Nanton Celebrity Branding Agency, NASCAR also offers some great marketing insights. Designed to increase sales and raise the Return On Investment of its corporate sponsors' ad spend, NASCAR promotes their content via social media, radio spots, and television commercials, as well as on merchandise, in team publicity and live events. Most notable of these are the races, and they can easily last up to three or four hours! Just think about that, what would it do for your business to have prospects view your logo and business name go round and round their TV screen, for three to four hours over the course of thirty-eight races in ten months? A visible repetition, or at least a good one, is a powerful marketing tool for building relationship and customer loyalty.

THE NASCAR RULE FOR MARKETING

We honestly can't remember where we heard it, but at one point someone told us about an axiom that says for every dollar that a company spends on sponsoring a team, driver, or putting their logo on a car, that company should be prepared to spend an equal dollar on *promoting their sponsorship with NASCAR.*

So, when branding a company alongside of NASCAR, that company should be willing to invest an equal amount of resources on marketing the fact that they are involved with NASCAR. The repetition and brand recognition inherent in this marketing strategy is a powerful principle for growing any business. This strategy will ensure that sponsors will get the greatest return from their marketing investment, and that consumers will have the company's brand name at top of mind. Basically, the NASCAR sponsorship money is building brand awareness and recognition, but it takes an equal amount of money to motivate a prospect to actually do something with that recognition.

We believe this is a really good analogy for the global influencers we work with as well. We often tell our clients that if they're going to write a best-selling book, be featured in Big Print Media Campaigns or have their story told on TV shows broadcast across the country, then it's a good idea to have an equal if not greater, amount of resources committed to marketing that initiative.

And we believe this strategy fits perfectly with our Celebrity Branding® use of the Business Trifecta®. The Business Trifecta® employs an unbeatable combination of media, marketing, and PR that creates visibility, establishes credibility, and effectively sells who you are and what you do. All three elements need to be used in order to build a stable brand that successfully sells your services.

LEVERAGE EXPOSURE TO GAIN MORE EXPOSURE

Much like the platform that NASCAR provides to their sponsors, clients who are seen in our major media outlets such as FOX, NBC, and CBS affiliates, or who are featured in national publications like *The Wall Street Journal* and *USA Today*, benefit the most when they leverage their exposure in marketing campaigns to drive revenue. This is how we help clients turn their Celebrity Expert® status into dollars for their business.

So, when clients come to us wanting to become a best-selling author, then of course we can help them with that. But we also try to encourage them to be thinking about how they are going to invest the same amount of time, energy and effort into marketing that project, in order to ensure the greatest possible return on their advertising and to build their business. Just by doing something that is a branding and positioning tool, much like a team's NASCAR sponsorship, writing a best-selling book on Amazon, or even sponsoring a local theatre or community event for that matter, the best success requires a plan for how you're going to get your message in front of the right market, and how you will monetize that new platform as well.

In essence what we are describing is leveraging your celebrity and media exposure to gain more brand awareness and build upon your existing market base. It goes back to the Business Trifecta® and using high quality media to build celebrity and expert credibility, which lends itself to more successful PR and effective direct marketing.

But we have found that most people don't take that into consideration when they take on a new project like this, or to share their story with the world and to build their business. The Celebrity Branding Agency® can help you build that credibility and status as the go-to Celebrity Expert® in your field, and we enjoy seeing our clients get great results because of that. But how much more of a return could they see if they had a plan in place to actively promote that Celebrity Expert status the way that NASCAR advises companies that sponsor with them to also promote the fact that they sponsor a car and team.

It's interesting, Tad Geschickter, the owner of JTG-Daugherty Racing, the team that fields the Monster Energy NASCAR Cup Series cars driven by AJ Allmendinger and Chris Buescher recently said on the Marketing Smarts podcast, that "One of the more fun things to do with sponsorship is to bring a new brand or a new product to market, where you have to create trial and awareness at the same time. I think events, whether they be NASCAR or street festivals or summer concert tours, are a great way to do that."

RECOGNITION CREATES BRAND AWARENESS FOR NEW CUSTOMERS

It's the same for the game-changing brands, inspired companies and global influencers that we work with. When they effectively *market their marketing*, they have the same opportunity to disrupt their respective industries and position themselves as the elite ThoughtLeaders® that they are, in each of their specific niches.

Like anything in business, our clients have to ask themselves if they are prepared to make the same amount of time and financial commitment necessary, once the project is completed, in order to leverage the guaranteed media coverage, marketing platform and PR utilized, to its fullest extent.

Some of the ways that our Celebrity Experts are able to leverage their status include:

1. Keeping a consistent image on all visual material, business cards, websites and other marketing collateral, with the *"As Seen On"* moniker.

2. Hosting a seminar when you give your Amazon best-

selling book away as a complementary resource to qualified business leads – after they complete an appointment request with you.

3. Publishing a monthly or weekly e-zine newsletter as a way to build and nurture your email list and reinforce your Celebrity Expert status in the byline.

4. Guest posting on a leading blog in your industry and directing readers back to your homepage to download a free report through an email opt-in.

5. Partnering with another Celebrity Expert® in a complementary, but non-competitive field. For example, if you're a financial advisor, consider doing an affiliate agreement with a tax professional who shares your same business philosophy and values alignment. Then you can both cross-market to each other's client list through direct mail with an irresistible offer, accompanied by a strong recommendation letter.

SHARE YOUR CELEBRITY EXPERT® STATUS TO HELP MORE PEOPLE

These are just a handful of ways to market your Celebrity Expert status with the same momentum as companies that sponsor with NASCAR. Remember, people process information differently. So be sure to share your Celebrity status across multiple media and marketing channels. Just like companies that sponsor with NASCAR actively promote their partnership via different outlets, be prepared to leverage your credibility as a Celebrity Expert on multiple fronts. Doing so will create brand loyalty and recognition for you and your business.

A strong Celebrity Brand and personality will help prospective customers quickly identify you as the only logical choice to meet their needs. The repetition of presenting your Core Story across multiple platforms will help to keep you and your services top of mind in the client's head. And the relationship your market will feel through your promotion will give a sense of omnipresence. Doing so will help to reinforce customer retention and make new referrals easier for your customer base to send your way.

For some of our clients, it's the content creation part of our projects that they find to be really fun. And for others, it's the marketing part that they live for. But the clients that we see who get the greatest return on becoming a Celebrity Expert, find ways to continually use their celebrity exposure to gain more media attention and publicity, and as a result, they ultimately get more business.

About JW

JW Dicks, Esq., is a Business Development Attorney, a *Wall Street Journal* Best-Selling Author®—who has authored over 47 books—and a 2 x Emmy® Award-Winning Executive Producer.

JW is an XPRIZE Innovation Board member, Chairman of the Board of the National Academy of Best-Selling Authors®, Board Member of the National Association of Experts, Writers and Speakers® and Board Member of the International Academy of Film Makers®.

JW is the CEO of DNAgency, an Inc. 5000 Multi Media Company that represents over 3,000 clients in 65 countries. He has been quoted on business and financial topics in national media such as *USA Today, The Wall Street Journal, Newsweek, Forbes, CNBC.com,* and *Fortune Magazine Small Business.*

Considered a ThoughtLeader® and curator of information, JW has co-authored books with legends like Jack Canfield, Brian Tracy, Tom Hopkins, Dr. Nido Qubein, Steve Forbes, Richard Branson, Michael Gerber, Dr. Ivan Misner, and Dan Kennedy. He is the Publisher of *ThoughtLeader® Magazine.*

JW is called the "Expert to the Experts" and has appeared on business television shows airing on ABC, NBC, CBS, and FOX affiliates around the country, and coproduces and syndicates a line of franchised business television shows such as *Success Today, Wall Street Today, Hollywood Live,* and *Profiles of Success.*

JW and his wife of forty-seven years, Linda, have two daughters, four granddaughters and two Yorkies. He is a sixth-generation Floridian and splits his time between his home in Orlando and his beach house on Florida's west coast.

About Nick

An Emmy Award-Winning Director and Producer, Nick Nanton, Esq., produces media and branded content for top thought leaders and media personalities around the world. Recognized as a leading expert on branding and storytelling, Nick has authored more than two dozen Best-Selling books (including the *Wall Street Journal* Best-Seller, *StorySelling™*) and produced and directed more than 50 documentaries, earning 5 Emmy Awards and 18 nominations. Nick speaks to audiences internationally on the topics of branding, entertainment, media, business and storytelling at major universities and events.

As the CEO of DNA Media, Nick oversees a portfolio of companies including: The Dicks + Nanton Agency (an international agency with more than 3000 clients in 65 countries), Dicks + Nanton Productions, Ambitious.com and DNA Films. Nick is an award-winning director, producer and songwriter who has worked on everything from large scale events to television shows with the likes of Steve Forbes, Ivanka Trump, Sir Richard Branson, Rudy Ruettiger (inspiration for the Hollywood Blockbuster, *RUDY*), Brian Tracy, Jack Canfield (*The Secret*, creator of the *Chicken Soup for the Soul* Series), Michael E. Gerber, Tom Hopkins, Dan Kennedy and many more.

Nick has been seen in *USA Today, The Wall Street Journal, Newsweek, BusinessWeek, Inc. Magazine, The New York Times, Entrepreneur® Magazine, Forbes, FastCompany,* and has appeared on ABC, NBC, CBS, and FOX television affiliates across the country as well as on CNN, FOX News, CNBC, and MSNBC from coast to coast.

Nick is a member of the Florida Bar, a member of The National Academy of Television Arts & Sciences (Home to the EMMYs), Co-founder of The National Academy of Best-Selling Authors®, and serves on the Innovation Board of the XPRIZE Foundation, a non-profit organization dedicated to bringing about "radical breakthroughs for the benefit of humanity" through incentivized competition, best known for its Ansari XPRIZE which incentivized the first private space flight and was the catalyst for Richard Branson's Virgin Galactic. Nick also enjoys serving as an Elder at Orangewood Church, working with Young Life, Downtown Credo Orlando, Entrepreneurs International and rooting for the Florida Gators with his wife, Kristina, and their three children,

Brock, Bowen and Addison.

Learn more at:
- www.NickNanton.com
- www.CelebrityBrandingAgency.com

CHAPTER 6

THE POWER FORMULA
THE SIMPLE SIX SUCCESS RECIPE

BY ANTHONY CALIENDO

THIS IS WHAT OUR PARENTS SAID...

Be smart. Get a good education. Have a good head on your shoulders. Settle down. Seek stability. Be a good person. Add a dash of religion, stir in a little bit of pleasure and a lot of patience and long-suffering and that's it – those were the ingredients to create a successful and rewarding life, according to most Baby Boomer parents. For those that know me know that my parents were a little more, let's say, "unconventional" in their approach. I knew what other parents told their kids and I watched enough TV to see how "ideal" parents steered the family. Meanwhile, back at the Caliendo's, I had a Grandpa that asked me, "Son, why are you even going to school?" I had a Dad and tons of uncles who had street smarts and business smarts but went totally left on the notion of "be a good person." And I had a Mother who struggled to create stability in our lives and had all of the right ideas, but somehow, while observing her scrap to survive day-in and day-out, the message was all but lost. So, what do you think I did?

First, I knew who I was and what I wanted to become. Figuring that out was simple for me – maybe not so simple for others, but that part was never an obstacle for me because winning was in my DNA. I have what I call a *Distinctive Nature to Achieve*. But the real challenge was learning how to tune out all the bu-----t and stop comparing myself to other people and their standards of "measuring up." I was different and not-so-normal, in a good way. So, I knew very early in life that the cookie cutter approach to success would never satisfy me nor would it lead me to big wins. I knew I was a leader. I knew I was destined for great things, so after a while, I quit waiting around for others to give me a shot in order to prove it.

So, this is what I did – I became a master "mixologist," sifting through the mixed messages and using my own instincts to create all of the right conditions leading to my own power and success; the perfect recipe. And over the years as a successful entrepreneur, this is how I did it: through *FAILURE, SELF-AWARENESS, DESIRE, OPTIMISM, KNOWLEDGE* and *STRATEGY.* My secret sauce that binds the recipe together is 1 part genetic and 2 parts experience – I'm a Caliendo after all. I make the "Sunday Gravy" at my house. My recipe for success is similar to my Sunday Gravy – fresh and simple – using only a few of the best quality ingredients which pair well together. And that's my approach to success, combining the best, most effective practices that allow me to score time and time again.

It all simmers down to **THE POWER FORMULA: THE SIMPLE SIX SUCCESS RECIPE:**

1. **FAILURE**. This is your main ingredient in the recipe. Why? Because experiencing failure is the only way you can perfect the recipe – to be creative and discover which ingredients work and which don't. You have to view failures as steps in the success process – stepping stones, notches, rungs in the ladder to up-leveling your game and improving your life. Thanks to Google, social media and memes, we're now all aware that it took Thomas Edison 1,000 tries before successfully inventing the light bulb. He didn't see them as

1,000 failures, he saw them as 1,000 experiments and he kept on adding, taking away, tasting and sampling before he found the exact ingredients to make that 'damn light bulb' work. So, this is how you should approach it: don't scrap the idea of failure, scrap the *fear*. Get rid of your fear of failing. ACCEPT that you're going to fail and if you have the right mindset – knowing that your fails are opportunities to fine tune the process and smooth out the lumps in the gravy – you'll know exactly what to do and what not to do to create more gravy for yourself, your business and your family.

2. **SELF-AWARENESS.** Knowing who you are and what drives you are big indicators of becoming self-aware. But that's not what I'm talking about. What I'm talking about is being able to look in the mirror and be crystal clear on your strengths and your weaknesses – removing all of the filters and stripping yourself down to bare bones. Becoming totally self-aware can be a painful process, probably because a lot us can't handle the truth. But it's a very necessary ingredient in the recipe because it is the key to discovering and eliminating patterns that keep preventing you from reaching next level in business and in life. I like to say, "if you do what you've always done, you get what you've always gotten." If you keep doing the same s--t and expect different results, over and over again, that means you're not owning up to what role *YOU* play in repeat fails (yes, I said fails). Let me be clear: the hallmark way to becoming self-aware is through failure because here's your opportunity to self-audit. Stop taking the long route. If you suck at something, own it, delegate it and then try again using a different angle; take ego out of the mix and add a dollop of reality.

3. **DESIRE.** Become obsessed. Simply, this is your hunger, your thirst and the thing that makes you want to satisfy your cravings each and every day. I talk a lot about having passion, dedication and courage in order to achieve success. Now let me explain the difference. In order to create the

vision, you have to have some kind of passion for what it is that you envision yourself achieving (money, power, respect, love). Passion inspires you to dream big. But once you create the vision, now you have to have the desire, focus and put relentless action behind it in order to actually achieve those dreams. Passion creates the vision. Desire executes it. Desire is the yeast in the dough which makes it rise. Get it?

4. **OPTIMISM.** A person's actions, reactions and subsequent choices that they make are activated by thought. That makes thought a very powerful energy and an extremely potent ingredient. However, thought comes in different varieties – not all are safe and suitable for the success recipe. As you create and go about executing your vision, experiencing failures and hitting that reset button, optimism is the spice that drives you and sustains your confidence. Right? Think about it. If thought drives your beliefs, which drives your behaviors, which drives your outcomes, and you're constantly pumping negative energy into those thoughts, what effect would that have on your actions? It definitely won't feed your desire, and that vision you created? "Fuhgeddaboudit." There's no passion without optimism and no big dreams without optimism. No Sunday Gravy without plum tomatoes. When you experience those fails, optimism drives you to reset, switch gears and push forward while predicting the best outcomes but here's the trick: optimism, not delusion. If you fold in the right amount of self-awareness, then you can keep delusion at bay.

5. **KNOWLEDGE.** If you're the smartest person in the room, then you're in the wrong room. Do not let ego convince you that you've mastered all of the lessons that life and business have to teach you. One cannot evolve in life, in business or as an individual without constantly learning, Grasshopper. And once again, one sure fire way to gain knowledge is through failure – see why it's the main ingredient in the recipe? Failure forces you to evaluate where the missing link

was in the process and to run it back, but this time, with new knowledge and insight to perfect your process.

In my book, *The Sales Assassin: Master Your Black Belt in Sales*, I talk about mental preparedness, I talk about investing in yourself, I talk about shifting the paradigm within the organization. All of these equate to acquiring and applying new knowledge. Especially when the business landscape is constantly changing, you have to stay on top of your game and keep leveling up. The market won't wait for you. Neither will life. So, constantly seek knowledge and extract it from all sources possible – from studying successful people to learning from your kids. Our kids, believe it or not, have an incredible pulse on what the market dictates, so who best to learn from when you're crafting your marketing strategy? Point is this: without a constant flow of new information and fresh ideas, your recipe will get stale.

6. **STRATEGY.** This is your GPS; this is how you 'nav' to your destination. You must employ strategy in all aspects of your life and in business. The tastiest strategies become your blueprint to leveraging your relationships, mapping out your goals, and designing a master plan that contains all of your moves to maintain and consistently up-level. Believe it or not, you're strategizing all of the time to achieve whatever it is that you set out to accomplish, whether it's personal or professional. But what happens when you encounter plot twists and unexpected detours in the road? The success recipe calls for higher quality ingredients within the strategy that contain keen senses and killer instinct. In business, you have to be able to spot trends, anticipate unexpected change and know how to farm out any and all opportunity for your benefit. Adding my brand of strategy gives you the edge and ability to stay one step ahead. So now, you've not only crafted the vision, you're a Visionary!

I wrote an article a few years ago called, "Mixing the Perfect Sales Cocktail." In it I laid out the alchemy for closing deals and scoring wins time and time again – using five simple key ingredients:

1) Sell yourself: *You're the product.*
2) Make your prospect comfortable: *Make them want to engage with you.*
3) Master "The Art of Asking Questions without Asking": *Eliminate the defense and learn how to listen.*
4) Isolate your buyer's hot spots: *Create value, need and solutions.*
5) Recognize the emotional drivers and negotiate accordingly: *Tune in to identify buying signals.*

Using that simple strategy, sales suddenly becomes less complex because you recognize that sales is "all about your desire to sell and their desire to buy." My Simple Six Success Recipe follows the same theory. Take the complexity out of the formula. Real talk. Now, of course, you're going to sample several different recipes – ones that include ingredients like determination, ambition, confidence, courage, resourcefulness, intuition – the list goes on. But when taste testing, think about it this way: you already have these things otherwise I bet you wouldn't be reading this book and my chapter. To bounce back from failure, you need insurmountable determination. To become self-aware, courage helps you face the truth. To activate your desire, ambition is key. To keep an optimistic outlook, you have to have confidence that the future is bright. When seeking knowledge, resourcefulness helps you find information and apply it immediately. And, no doubt, you can't become a strategic visionary without the intuition to navigate. The Power Formula is for those who are ready to up their game and compete with other gamers, right?

THE POWER FORMULA: THE SIMPLE SIX SUCCESS RECIPE is easy to follow but the prep time depends on the chef. If you're a young entrepreneur just starting out, have some patience with yourself and know that success is not always instant. Most success stories have years of grinding with blood, sweat and tears behind them. My firm belief is you will not achieve sustainable success without hard work and resilience. But if you're a veteran like me who's been in the game, and you're reading this chapter, perhaps my simple recipe will help you put it all into perspective and finally achieve the success you deserve – in one yummy bite.

Dream Big! Achieve your dreams!

About Anthony

The business world changes around us with relentless speed and intensity. It takes great vision to not only see these changes, but to also anticipate and react with the tenacity to sustain success.

Few business leaders possess the innate skills to maneuver the modern-day challenges of today's business. Anthony Caliendo is one of these self-made men, an entrepreneur and corporate visionary. To thrive in business and beyond, Anthony learned to project and understand the trends and dynamic forces that shape business and to always move swiftly and strategically.

Anthony is a professional salesman, marketing machine, and sales leadership coach with supersensory sales skills, proven success in sales strategy and corporate leadership, and has generated hundreds of millions in sales revenues; he trained thousands of sales pros in various industries over 25 years to define him as the Ultimate Sales Assassin Master! Today he is a motivational sales speaker and author of the international best-selling, multi-award winning book, *The Sales Assassin: Master Your Black Belt in Sales.* He was also a featured Thought Leader® and co-author of the book *Cracking the Code to Success* with Brian Tracy.

Anthony discovered his entrepreneurial instincts early in life. At 18, he became the youngest manager at that time to oversee Chicago Health Clubs and built the World Gyms with Arnold Schwarzenegger. Afterwards, Caliendo went on Wall Street as a stock broker where his instincts and thirst for sales domination accelerated. Achieving financial success on Wall Street and other business ventures, Anthony mastered the art of branding when he became known as "The Main Man" in the mortgage business, architect of one of South Florida's most successful mortgage and real estate companies and an on-air celebrity. In 2008, during one of the worst economic downturns, Anthony reinvented himself and became the #1 Italian Cheese Salesman in the USA known as the "The Big Cheese" at 1-800-BIGCHEESE, directing his manufacturer's national and global expansion.

Anthony continues to keeps his sales and entrepreneurial skills sharp and in full practice. In 2017, he revived "The Main Man" and 1-800-THEMAINMAN, and is one of South Florida's premier business broker's, successfully listing and selling millions in businesses for sale.

His outrageous and relentless mentality drove Anthony to construct a fail-proof sales model encompassing specific skillsets and concepts that became the foundation of sales training. The motivational themes of his sales experience inspired him to write *The Sales Assassin* and become a sales motivational speaker and sales coach to salespeople in all industries.

Anthony has showcased his sales strategies on radio and on CBS, NBC, ABC and FOX and a contributing writer in industry mags including *Salesforce, Small Biz Daily, The Canadian Business Journal, Focus Magazine, TK Business Magazine, AMA Playbook, In Business Magazine* and *Digital Journal.*

Anthony lives and works in South Florida with his wife, Lynette and their eight children.

To connect with Anthony or for more information on motivational speaking, coaching services or media opportunities, please visit:

- Website: www.thesalesassassin.com
- Telephone: + 1-561-265-1405
- Email: info@thesalesassassin.com
- Facebook.com/TheSalesAssassin
- Twitter.com/1SalesAssassin
- LinkedIn: https://www.linkedin.com/in/anthonycaliendo1

CHAPTER 7

THREE HIDDEN FACTS ABOUT REAL ESTATE
THAT CAN CHANGE YOUR FINANCIAL FUTURE!

BY BILL FARRAND

I want to thank you for buying this book. I have a lot of good stuff to cover and I have put together an outstanding, honest-to-goodness chapter on how you can ethically copy a simple real estate niche and hit your financial freedom number. Even if you've never done a real estate deal before.

I'm going to reveal some things I've discovered, and I'm also going to let you in on three little secrets that can change your financial future. My goal is that by the end of this thing, you'll say, "You know what…this was really valuable to me…this guy is great…he has helped me"…and you'll go out and test this stuff on your own. My sincere hope is it will work for you and you'll let me know all about it.

The purpose of this information is to show you how you can ethically copy a simple real estate niche and get to your financial freedom number, even if you've never done a real estate transaction. I'm going to show you how to do this by walking you through the process I use to generate multiple six-figures in profit for me and my clients.

So, with that said, let me tell you who this is for, because this is definitely not for everybody. This is not a get-rich-quick thing, you really have to actually be willing to put in the work. This is about a specific niche in the real estate business and if you're not willing to work, this is not the right place for you.

If you're looking for the latest get-rich-quick magic snake oil, or some fast, easy way to get rich overnight, you're not going to enjoy this at all. Everything I'm going to show you does require work, and it's for real people who are in real estate already, or people who want to get started in real estate.

First of all, my results are not typical, and this does not translate into how much money you're going to make. I have no idea what you're going to make. I'm typing on a computer screen right now, so everything I'm telling you today or anytime I'm referencing income figures – it's for informational purposes only. It is not some hidden income claim...I'm not that guy! So, if you're looking for the information on how you can make a million dollars sitting at your kitchen table in your underwear...it's not me!

Your success is 100% dependent on your effort, and I can tell you right now, this always takes more work than we ever anticipate. I've been doing it for 25 years and there's no easy button. My results and the hypothetical examples in this chapter are for illustrative purposes only. And most people who get "How-To-make-money" training, don't make any money.

I don't know why that is. I guess maybe it's the same reason that people who buy weight loss stuff don't lose weight and don't have a beach body. It's not Beach Body's fault they didn't do the workouts and follow the program.

So those are the facts, and if you're looking for the easy button… you can just leave now. For everyone else, who hasn't been scared off by my upfront "NO B.S." and brutally honest dose of reality, let's get to work…

First and foremost, I want you to be successful, I want you to get to your financial freedom number and I want you to get there as soon as possible.

So, let me ask you a question. If you were going to learn something new, which would you prefer:

A. The "How To" manual – Here's the Manual…good luck… hope you can figure it out.
B. The "Do-It-**With**-Me/Show-Me" method – you work with an experienced individual who walks you through all the steps necessary to reach your end goal.
C. The "Do-It-**For**-Me" method – this is when you just pay somebody a whole bunch of money and they do it for you.

Which one are people wanting more than the others? If you said "B" – "Do It **With** Me" – you're right. And that is why I put this information together. After 25 years in the business, I've discovered some things and you might not like them, but stay with me. It's all going to make sense and come together.

The first thing I discovered is that being a landlord is all hyped up. There are more books and programs about land lording than I care to count. You know how the story goes…buy a house…rent it out…tenant pays your mortgage…you make $300, $400, $500 in passive income.

What they don't tell you about is all the maintenance, repairs, clean outs and/or court cases for eviction. If you've ever bought a "How To" manual about lead generation for your real estate business, one of the ways in the "How To" manual is…go to eviction court and find all the burnt out landlords. Make them an offer to buy their house that's been totally trashed by their tenant who just got evicted. Land lording is not for me...been there, done that.

Next thing I discovered is wholesaling and rehabbing or fix-and-flip is nothing more than another *full-time job*. You're constantly working yourself out of a job. Always on the hunt for the next deal. Getting all or most of your lowball offers rejected and having to settle for a mediocre deal, just so you can have a deal to make payroll...been there, done that too! You end up constantly chasing down contractors to get the job started and completed. The electrician blames the plumber, ...the plumber blames the drywaller, ... etc., etc., etc.

What I also discovered is there are plenty more people who are currently renting but who would much rather own a house, and this is where you can really be profitable. I discovered this the hard way, and I'm going to give you permission to cheat and ethically copy me.

Here's the hard way – run a bunch of ads, spend a small fortune on mailings and put out bandit signs (I never had any real success with – "I buy Houses All Cash.").

The owners who typically respond to your bandit signs or ads are not selling rent-ready homes. So, now you can try to wholesale it to another rehabber guy, if you can get it on the cheap.

Perhaps maybe you're the fix-and-flip guy and now you're going to need to get it funded, make all the repairs and upgrades, and you need to get it done on budget – which never happens, and anyone who says different, is either lying, or has never done a rehab before. I'll never forget a project we did and lost $30,000 and it still pisses me off.

The next hard way is to turn it into a rental and collect $500 per month cash flow. What they don't tell you about is all the heart ache and grief. Are you familiar with the term T and T? It has some different meanings...Tenants and Toilets...Tenants and Trash...again...been there, done that.

Over the past few years I've discovered a better way, and I didn't have to waste a lot of time and money.

There are three hidden facts of real estate you need to believe in:

- **Fact #1:** People paying $1,200 to rent would rather pay $1,200 to own.
- **Fact #2:** There is a line of renters, ready and willing to become owners.
- **Fact #3:** The mathematical formula works every time to establish value.

It's not that difficult. You don't need a fancy calculator. All you need is a basic calculator and you don't need to understand Einstein's theory of Relativity in order for this to work. Where this gets screwed up all the time is people try and make it difficult.

- Do you believe that people paying $1,200 to rent would rather pay $1,200 to own?
- Do you believe that a majority...a large majority...would rather own vs rent?
- Do you believe there is a line of renters ready and willing to become owners?
- Do you believe the mathematical formula works every time to establish value?

Would you like to know this formula?

Here's the formula...
1. The rental income minus taxes and insurance equals principle and interest payment.
2. Principle and interest payment x 110 equals the loan balance/ mortgage...stay with me and yes, I'm going to give a real example.

3. The loan balance + 10% equals the seller-financed value.

Do you understand how we established the seller-financed value based on the rent?

The Seller Financed Value is not the appraised value, it's not some broker price opinion, it's not a comparative market analysis, it's not the tax assessment value. Yes, these numbers matter but they don't determine the Seller Financed Value.

Your #1 asset is being able to establish the seller-financed value and knowing your exit price. Not every property on the market is going to fit this formula, but once you plug in the numbers, the formula will tell you the seller-financed value, and then you decide if you want to pass on it or take it down. I'm going to start putting real numbers into this formula so it's more clear.

Here's our seller finance value formula... rent minus the taxes and insurance...times 110 plus 10% equals the seller finance value.

Let's assume in our hypothetical example we have a 3 bedroom, 1½ bath home that has a rental price of $1,200 and the monthly taxes and insurance combined is $200.

$1,200 - $200 for tax and insurance = $1,000 for the principal and interest payment...pretty simple math, right.

Now we have $1,000 which is our principal and interest payment times 110 which equals $110,000...without getting all crazy...if we plug $110,000 loan value at 10% interest for 25 years into a financial calculator, the exact monthly payment is $999.57. Now, do you see how simple and almost perfect this calculation works? We're not done yet.

Now that we know our loan balance is $110,000, we want to add an additional 10%, which in this scenario would be $11,000, which brings us to our seller finance value of $121,000. 10% is what we're looking for as a down payment. To silence all the naysayers and haters out there… yes, there are people out there with 10% available for down payment. Have I accepted less than 10% in the past? Yes. Every deal is different, every buyer is different, you are the bank and you decide if it's a go or a no go. We determined that seller-financed value is $121,000. Let's also assume we purchased this property for $65,000.

We sold this home with seller financing for $121,000… our end buyer paid $10,250 for down payment. Yes, this is only 8% down. We created a Note and Mortgage for $110,750 at 10% interest for 25 years, and the monthly payment is $1,006.39. Yes, we are creating a new note and mortgage. We are the bank, we can change the interest, change the number of years, it's whatever we agree to.

Now if this loan goes out the full term, meaning they don't sell the house or refinance it with a different lender (which is perfectly ok). We collected $10,250 for the down payment, we're collecting $1,006 a month for 25 years (or 300 months) and our total revenue is $312,167.

Remember we bought this house for $65,000 so our potential total net profit is $247,167. This deal was put together almost 3 years ago, and the buyer hasn't missed a payment.

Does every deal work like this?... No.

Have we had to drop the hammer on some people and foreclose? ... Yes.

Do you see how and why this business model is successful?

We bought a house for $65,000 sold it for $121,000, collected $10,250 for a down payment, and we're collecting $1,000 a month, all because we said yes…to seller financing. If the kitchen faucet starts leaking…not our problem…if the furnace or AC unit quits working…not our problem…

We Are The Bank! ☺

About Bill

Bill Farrand is one of the country's leading real estate experts. Bill has owned multiple real estate companies, written three real estate books, he is a former licensed realtor, he has a team of real estate and marketing professionals with over a combined $1Billion dollars of real estate transactions and he is also a member of: "The National Association of Experts, Writers & Speakers."

(Bill says…"I always love the "about me" section like this because they're written in the third person, even though they're typically written by the individual.")

So after Bill Farrand made several attempts to sound smarter than he really is by writing about himself in the third person, he quickly abandoned that approach and decided to write this page like it was a letter to a friend.

Which in many ways, it is. Anyway – You're probably wondering… *Is This Guy Worth My Time And Attention?* For most readers, the answer is NO.

BILL SAYS HERE'S WHY:

#1. I cannot help you get rich quick.

For some reason, people equate "REAL ESTATE" to "get rich quick." I get it. That's what attracted me to real estate. I thought it would be easy money and I'd have thousands coming in every month on autopilot. Well, it wasn't easy money. I do have a consistent revenue coming in every month, but it took lots of work and perseverance to get here. And it still takes work to keep it all running. So if you're not prepared to invest money and make the commitment, I'm not your guy.

#2. If you don't want to invest money, you're not going to like what I do.

Here's why I'm telling you this. Start going down the "No Money Down" rabbit hole, and you'll see all kinds of ads and articles about free houses, how to get rich quick, and all kinds of hype on the "latest loopholes" for "gaming the system."

Does some of it work? Yes, in the short term. But if you rely on that, you don't have a business. You have an income stream that's supported by an unsustainable gimmick. And that is a waste of time.

#3. If you're looking for "The Easy Way" I don't want to help you.

It's important you understand what I'm telling you. I can help you, I'm capable of it, but I refuse to do it.

Why? Because when I hear someone say, "What's the easy way?", what I'm really hearing is, "I'm not fully invested in the long term success of my business and I am therefore not fully committed to the long term success of my business." And that really translates to "I don't want to work." Look, real estate investing requires work.

Yes, when it's all up and running, it can be just like you imagined: Passive Income and money while you sleep. But that takes work to create and it takes work to maintain.

For more information on Bill, please visit: www.BillFarrand.com

CHAPTER 8

GETTING YOUR AFFAIRS IN ORDER

THE NEED FOR FINANCIAL ADVOCACY IN THE MODERN ERA

BY GREG DuPONT, CFP®, JD

The broker is not your friend. He is more like a doctor who charges patients on how frequently they change their medicine.
~ Warren Buffett

The sad reality is that most consumers are likely to receive bad, misleading, or outdated information when they look for financial guidance. Whether it is being left unaware of the high fees that they are being charged, being sold products that are not appropriate for their needs or being convinced to leave their life savings at risk in the market, the modern consumer has become the prey to this predatory business.

WHAT'S A DILIGENT CONSUMER TO DO? THE ANSWER: FIND A FINANCIAL ADVOCATE

There are people in the financial services industry who hold themselves to a higher standard than the industry imposes. They are called Fiduciaries. While this is a step in the right direction, I believe an even higher standard is warranted: that of a financial advocate.

The standard a financial advocate holds themselves to is one of providing leadership and doing what is best for you. A financial advocate is uniquely qualified to craft customized financial strategies based on your individual needs and desires and takes on the duty to protect you from the financial services industry by bringing a multi-disciplinary approach to your finances.

BECOMING A FINANCIAL ADVOCATE:

I became a financial advocate because of what I have witnessed in my law practice. Over the years I have met many financial advisors. I have seen the good that can be done when a consumer has a capable, trustworthy advisor. However, I have also seen that far too few of those relationships exist.

I made my decision to become a financial advocate while I was working on an estate dispute case. Sitting in a deposition related to that case, it struck me that while the family I was representing had estate planning attorneys, financial advisors, and accountants, they did not have a single advisor that they trusted to call upon when the now-deceased mother decided to change her estate plan.

When she decided to change her estate plan, she called her son. He made all the changes his mom wanted; unfortunately, he did all the *wrong* things in the process of changing the plan, which allowed the charities his mother had previously supported to contest what he had done. Unfortunately, this resulted in hundreds of thousands of dollars in legal fees as well as millions of dollars lost to the family.

In reflecting on this story, I realized that what caused this great loss for the family was the fact that they did not have an advisor whom they felt they could pick up the phone and call to have these issues taken care of for them.

I noticed that in the modern estate planning process, the consumer was being treated as a series of transactions by the various parties, and I decided there had to be a better way. I set out to define that better way through a process I call "integrated estate planning."

I basically drew upon my training as a litigator and put the affiliated industries on trial. I dug in with the goal of protecting as many people as I could from this predatory business model. My research has reinforced my thesis that the legal, investment, and insurance industries have biases and structural flaws that leave the modern consumer exposed to undue risk at best, and subject to manipulation at worst.

THE THREE HIDDEN BIASES MOST HARMFUL TO INVESTORS

In my investigation of the industry, and after talking to hundreds of people, it has become apparent to me that, surprise, financial advisors are humans just like us. You see, the vast majority of people are prone to innate biases. In this industry, despite whatever perspective someone is coming from, whether primarily an investment or insurance background, they are going to be shaped by these biases. It's just human nature that we are all influenced by what we are exposed to on a day-to-day basis.

1. The Insurance Bias:

If an agent is coming from the insurance world, his or her company is constantly feeding them a narrative that insurance is in the client's best interest. If you don't believe that in your heart as an insurance agent, then you're not going to succeed in the business – you'll wash out quickly.

Agents who have succeeded in the business are true acolytes of the products to which they have grown accustomed. Now the problem for the consumer is that it is difficult to get good advice from an agent. This agent may or may not have the right solution for what they need or may not be qualified to give the advice that the client needs.

It's easy for an old-timer, who is established in the profession, to get complacent. And if they are a captive agent of a particular life insurance company they may be limited to their product line. What I've found in searching the industry is that thinking that one company always has the best solution for the consumer is like believing in a mythical unicorn.

There is so much competition in the marketplace and such great innovation taking place all the time, that if one is a captive agent of a particular company, then the fact is, they may not have all the tools in their toolbox. But these agents are going to sell what they have, or else they'll starve to death. This combination of an insurance agent's limited toolbox and the pressure on the agent to make a sale, is a bad situation for the consumer.

2. *The Investment Bias:*

Now if you look at the investment world, you'll see something very similar. In this case it is more pernicious because it often happens at a level that the consumer doesn't even recognize or fully understand.

For example, if an investment broker is at a company being supported by a good mutual fund family, then that broker can very easily be reduced to using the supporting mutual fund's particular product as a solution for every one of their clients' needs. While the advisor may not be overtly told to use this product, because that's prohibited by FINRA and other regulatory agencies, the subtle, hidden influence can be quite strong. For example, certain fees may be reduced if you have invested enough in a fund family; these are called "break points."

If an investor goes to a broad brokerage provider, the company may have arrangements with certain product providers and that influences them to push those particular products.

There are conflicting issues at play here. Arthur Levitt, a former investment broker and the longest serving chairman of the U.S. Securities and Exchange Commission, having served for 12 years, warned of these dangers to consumers. In 2002, Levitt wrote the national bestselling book, *Take on the Street: How to Fight for Your Financial Future* where, according to the July 22nd, 2007 Daily News & Analysis online article, Levitt "Revealed the inside secrets of how stock brokers on Wall Street fleece the retail investors who buy and sell stocks through them." Levitt writes, "They (brokers) want you to buy stocks you don't own and sell the ones you do, because that's how they make money for themselves and their firms. They earn commissions even when you lose money." Still, Levitt feels that there are a lot of:

"Good people stuck in a bad system, whose problems remain fourfold:

1. Some brokers are not trained well enough for the enormous task they are expected to carry out.

2. The system in which brokers operate is still geared toward volume selling, not giving objective advice.

3. To increase sales, firms use contests to get brokers to sell securities that investors may not need.

4. Branch-office managers and other supervisors who are paid commissions just like their brokers, have an incentive to push everyone to sell more and to turn a blind eye to questionable practices."

The true nature of the financial industry was vividly illustrated in their recent fight against the effort to impose the fiduciary "best interest" standard upon it.

The consumer never really knows if they're getting the straight story. After all, these brokers are first and foremost salesmen. What more savvy consumers do, is they look at using low cost conservative index funds and the magic process called "diversification." Diversification is the industry mantra and is alleged to protect you in good times and bad. Unfortunately, in recent market corrections it has not done that.

Diversification is simply the industry protecting itself. When the consumer is pushed into pretty pie charts showing that they are diversified, the industry declares that their risk tolerance is met. The advisor has satisfied this suitability standard and, as a result you can't sue the advisor for the recommendation. This is far below the best interest standard, which requires not just suitability, but that the advisor's proposals are in the client's best interest.

So how does a recommendation move from being "suitable" to being in your best interest? For one thing, the advisor has to disclose to the client all the fees that the client may not really understand. In many instances, those fees end up going back to the investment firm as inducement to sell the funds.

There are studies that show while the average mutual fund investor thinks they're paying around 1% in fees, they are actually paying more like 2.5% and these funds are still "suitable."

As a result of this whole suitability standard and use of pie charts regime is that the consumer will inevitably lose anywhere from 20%, 30%, or even up to 40% of their savings in a market correction. As long as the consumer was squeezed into that pie chart that met their suitability standard, the financial company that put them into that fund is protected, as is the advisor that put them there is as well.

This is why a financial advocate takes on the challenge of protecting your savings by using tactical investment methods, forward-looking due diligence, and safe money tools while the rest of the industry relies on hindsight and disclaimers to protect themselves.

3. *The Fee-only Bias:*

Then there's a third bias, and this is the bias from people that are in the movement to be as pure of a financial advisor as possible, that's a fee-only financial advisor. This bias ironically starts as the result of trying to overcome the insurance or investment bias.

As illustrated above, if you're an insurance or investment broker, you have to be a complete believer and acolyte in your industry to succeed.

If you are a successful agent in the investment world, then you are a true believer in the power of the market. If you are a believer in the power of the market, then you're not likely to give much consideration to other solutions that may be more in the best interest of the client.

And that's giving the benevolent view. The malevolent view says that if I'm an investment manager and my client says "Hey, I heard about this insurance solution called an indexed annuity and I've heard that this might make sense for me. Does it?" Well, consciously or unconsciously the investment manager tenses up because he doesn't make money off insurance solutions.

So, even if it makes sense for the family, helping them to sleep more peacefully at night, to carve out 25% – 30% of their savings, and to put it into a secure growth indexed product, that's going to have a direct impact on the advisor's ability to continue to maintain his own income.

There is potentially a subconscious bias against saying, "Yeah, that makes sense to do that." Unless the advisor is able to pull himself out of that way of thinking, it's very easy for him to stand behind the suitability norms of his own industry and the belief in the market as it currently stands, to continue to hold on to your money even if it is not in your best interest.

Similarly, if the conversation is with a financial advisor from the insurance world and you need guidance on investments, then the insurance agent is not likely to fully support an investment solution because he primarily makes his money from the sale of insurance products.

The movement toward independent fee only financial planning came in large part from an effort to address these biases by removing compensation for implementing the solutions from the equation. Under this approach, the consumer pays for a comprehensive plan and guidance to achieve their financial goals. One of the problems with this approach is cost. This approach is often too expensive for the client. Since the advisor cannot be compensated by commission or money management fees, the advisor has to charge a sufficient enough fee to keep in business. This fee may be too much for the consumer and as a result, the consumer does not get the information and guidance that is needed.

Another problem arises in the bias against the use of some tools such as insurance-based products that the fee-only planner may look at with disdain because of the commission element, but which nonetheless may be the right answer for the consumer.

A Fourth Model:
INTEGRATED ESTATE PLANNING AND FINANCIAL ADVOCACY

We have a fourth perspective, and that's the perspective of a truly unbiased financial advocate. Being a fiduciary, advocate, and leader in a process I call, "Integrated Estate Planning."

Drawing on all my experience throughout the last decade, I've created a proprietary, systematic process that is designed to take you from where you are in your financial life to where you want to be. I will walk with you hand-in-hand as a coach and leader, from whatever point we come together, whether it's when you are in your 20's, 30's, or 70's, it doesn't matter, to make sure that you receive independent, unbiased advice.

This guidance helps you learn the options and relevant solutions that are pertinent and available to you at that point in your life, and then to make the adjustments necessary to keep you on course as time goes on.

A simple summary for the Integrated Estate Planning model would be:

A. Meet the clients where they are (life stage, specific situation, etc.).

B. Provide financial advice that is free from product and industry bias and the leadership to pursue the client's unique financial goals.

C. Make course corrections as necessary to keep you on a path to your desired life, as those dreams inevitably change throughout life, in a systematic fashion.

This process protects you from going down the wrong paths and protects you from the negative influences and industry biases. A properly-trained lawyer is uniquely suited to fulfill this role as a true, financial advocate helping clients get their affairs in order and protecting them from the predatory practices of the financial service industry.

About Greg

Greg DuPont, CFP®, JD is a well-respected, Estate Planning Attorney and Financial Advisor, with 26 years of experience providing clients the legal and financial advice they need. Known as a trusted advocate for his clients' financial future, Greg helps clients receive unbiased advice for proper estate planning through his firm, DuPont Wealth Solutions.

After graduating from The Ohio State University with a Bachelor of Science in Finance and Accounting, Greg went on to complete his law degree at Capital University Law School, where he specialized in Estate Planning and Taxation.

As a fiduciary, Greg is committed to acting with his clients' best interest in mind, and upholds the highest ethical standards of integrity and true professionalism. His combination of financial, legal, and fee-based services ensure that his clients meet their financial goals with success.

Greg's extensive legal background has included services in business advising, commercial litigation and bankruptcy. He is honored to hold the esteemed financial designation of being a Certified Financial Planner®, and combines all of this unique experience to create custom solutions for his clients with his proprietary model of Integrated Estate Planning.

Born and raised a "Buckeye", Greg lives in Columbus, Ohio where he is happily married to his loving wife, Julia, and is a proud father to his daughter, Sophie. When he's not spending time with his family, serving clients as a trusted advisor, or staying abreast of the most current financial news, Greg loves to watch Ohio State Football.

Whether you are looking to build, protect, or transfer your wealth, Greg is happy to help you put an estate plan in place that will allow you the peace of mind of knowing that all your important financial affairs are in order.

You can connect with Greg on (LinkedIn/Facebook):

- Online at www.DuPontWealth.com
- Email: Greg@DupontWealth.com
- Phone: (614) 408 - 0004

CHAPTER 9

FIVE BEGINNERS TIPS TO START ACCOUNTING FOR YOUR BUSINESS

BY JACQUI YOU

You've started a business – Congratulations!!!

Then at some point, the cold realisation that you will need to keep financial records and report to the Authorities dawns on you – and the dread and procrastination begin!

Accounting isn't the most inspiring or exciting of subjects for most people. Being busy, not being sure what's required and a lack of confidence in our abilities, results in it constantly slipping towards the bottom of our "To-do" list, despite us constantly thinking, and maybe even mentioning to people, that we "really need to do something to sort out our accounting."

That works until a reporting deadline looms, and the penalties for non-compliance make it sufficiently compelling for us to tackle it. Then we have the added stress of even more time pressure on top of still not knowing what to do – aaaarghhh!!!

Let me tell you a secret – it doesn't have to be like this!

"Really?" I hear you cry, "do tell me more."

The ideal solution for most people would be for someone else to do it for them. Maybe the house-cleaning, clothes-washing, food-shopping and tidying-up fairies could have a word with the accounting ones? Seriously though, have a think about whether there is anyone in your life who could do it for you. Maybe a relative, friend, neighbour, or someone you know has the necessary skills, and would be willing to help.

If this isn't an option, you'll probably want something quick and easy that isn't going to cost too much, in time or money – while still giving you peace of mind that your accounting is being done properly – a method that ensures you are doing things correctly and keeping sufficient records to satisfy the Authorities. You'll also want to ensure you're claiming all the costs and expenses you're entitled to, and that things are organised efficiently to minimise your tax bill.

So, what do you have to do, and where do you begin?

1. Build a Team – "Team You!"

You are unique and have your own special talents and skills set. Play to your strengths and surround yourself with people and resources that cover your weaknesses, and those areas that you have little interest in. Concentrate on those roles that only you can fill – whether they're in your business, your family, relationships or social networks.

For the rest, delegate or outsource those necessary tasks that need expert knowledge, or that you have no appetite for. There's lots of help and resources available – both physically or virtually via the internet.

Do some research and identify what you need to know and where you can find the necessary information and skills.

Make it easy for yourself by asking people you know who have faced the same challenges. Read articles and books, listen to webinars and podcasts, or watch videos to educate yourself and find ideas to help you progress forward. You will find people who resonate with you, so include them in 'Team You!' and let their knowledge, ideas, trainings, and experience help you to 'get up to speed quickly'. Let them help you gain crucial knowledge and skills, show you what's possible, and inspire you!

2. Make some decisions

As with many things in life, there are lots of different ways to achieve your goals, and keeping Accounts is no different. Once you've done your research, you will have sufficient knowledge to make informed decisions about which options will best suit your enterprise, as well as you, as an individual.

Some of the questions you might ask to help you make these decisions are:

- Do I want to keep the books myself, or have someone else do them? Maybe a solution combining these two extremes is right for you?

- Who do I know with accounting knowledge/experience who could help me to either identify my next step, or maybe even do the Accounts?

- If I want to do some of the bookkeeping myself, how can I acquire the necessary skills and knowledge? Local or online courses, internet searches, YouTube videos, books, articles and online accounting services are just a few of the options available.

- Do I want the records kept manually or on a computer?

- If I choose to keep my records on a computer, do I want to use a spreadsheet or a bespoke software or service?

Once you have clarity on how you want to proceed, you can plan a way to acquire the necessary knowledge, skills or services – whether that is to learn or improve your own knowledge, or to choose someone to take care of your Accounting for you.

Once you are clear on what you want to achieve, and how, it is much easier to narrow down your options, clear out any unnecessary activities and focus on those actions that will move you forward towards your goals.

3. Choose a system

I am a huge fan of using systems to simplify life. Routine, mundane and repetitive tasks can be streamlined and automated, allowing them to be processed more efficiently, in less time, at lower cost and with fewer errors. Systems also allow you to 'brain dump' a lot of the information cluttering up your brain, freeing up valuable head space. This gives you time and space to concentrate on important things, be creative and do more of the things that give you joy.

I once worked in a company where those who reported to me would rather ask me questions than think for themselves. I'm sure you can understand why I wanted to empower them by making them more self-sufficient to free up my time – especially when the turnover increased from £20K to £2m almost overnight. We did this by introducing a series of systems with the aim of making me redundant. So, if I was to be hit by a bus, the systems would still operate, and the department continue to function with minimum disruption.

Not that I was planning to be hit by a bus. The point is that having a system makes your business less reliant on specific individuals. It also reduces the 'firefighting' inevitable crises require, as the potential for error reduces. Introducing systems has also allowed me to travel extensively, running my current Office remotely. Systems free up time and energy for more creative, productive and fulfilling activities – once the humdrum is taken care of.

Regardless of whether you decide to keep the books yourself, or have someone help you, you will need to keep all your receipts and invoices – for both the items and services you sell, and those that you buy into the business. Having a system will make this easier to do, keeping all your paperwork organised in one place.

It can be as simple as having a big envelope or folder that you put your invoices and receipts into. Or you may want to have a file that is divided into individual months with plastic pockets to keep the paperwork in. If you want to take it a step further, you can file with the most recent on the top or at the front. Alternatively, you may prefer to keep your records digitally on an electronic device. I would recommend dating them in YY/MM/DD format as it keeps them in date order.

Just having somewhere to put your receipts makes it easier for you. You won't have to remember where they are or keep thinking that you really need to put them somewhere safe rather than having them 'filed' in your pockets, wallet, handbag, car, different emails, or wherever else you've stuffed them! When you get a generic till receipt with little information, write yourself a reminder of what it was for, on it. This'll make your life easier when you need to analyse it.

Regarding receipts, get a receipt for everything! It's proof that you've spent the money. It's also more reliable than relying on your memory to make sure you claim all your expenses and minimise your tax bill. Who doesn't want that?

4. Little and often

Once a system is established, use it!

Make it easy for yourself. Don't waste precious time and effort 're-inventing the wheel' when you can just slip into a pre-prescribed system. Accounts, like your business, benefit from frequent and consistent attention. Rather than doing your accounts on the same frequency as your reporting deadlines, with the accompanying stress and time pressure that brings, deal with them in a more timely, methodical, and controlled way. This can be daily, weekly, or monthly, depending on the volume of transactions and what suits you. Quarterly or annually start to sound like reporting deadline timeframes – and we've already ascertained that's not good for your stress levels!

Doing your accounts in small chunks of time, more regularly, makes the process less daunting. It becomes more familiar, habit forming and more like second nature. 10 minutes a day is easier to find than nearly an hour a week, or 3½ hours a month – which starts to enter the realms of 'scary'!

If you had to fit in 3½ hours of accounting, how easy would it be to not do it and let it slide – until it's 7 hours at the end of next month – or a whopping 42 hours after a year – that's roughly a whole working week for accounting you'd have to fit in at the end of the year. That's a sobering thought! You'd probably have to 'relearn' the process each year; having forgotten what to do in the intervening year since you'd last done it! Not forgetting the worry and stress suffered during the year - you can see why it's a situation best avoided.

Prevention is better than cure – much better to do a little often; your accounts will be up to date and you'll be 'in control'. Think of the sense of achievement and satisfaction you'll have, not to mention the peace of mind it'll give you.

5. Just get started – NOW!

There is no better time to start than NOW! Just dive in and get started today.

Don't worry if you started your business a while back and have previous records to deal with. Introduce and implement a system today and use it. Then all future accounting records can be organised and dealt with promptly. Leaving only the existing previous outstanding records, that need to be organised, to get you up to date.

If you wait to go back and organise from the beginning, tackling it seems more daunting, and you may be tempted to put it off (sound familiar?). This increases the non-recorded items daily, allowing the 'problem' to grow bigger and bigger. Better to deal with it immediately and stop it in its tracks. Remove worry and stress instantly – simultaneously regaining peace of mind.

Don't wait until tomorrow, or next week – something may distract you, so it doesn't happen, and all your good intentions come to nothing. If there are genuine reasons why you can't do it now, give yourself a reasonable deadline and stick to it. Doing what you say you're going to do helps build integrity and self-belief, making you feel better about yourself.

Action is required for anything great to happen – we can know something in theory, but it is not until we apply it practically that we truly learn and understand it. Reading, learning, planning and preparing are all great disciplines, but in order for anything to happen, we must act.

ACT NOW!

We trust that these five tips have taken away some of your fear of accounting – fear of not knowing enough, or doubting whether you can do it. You are more than capable of doing your own accounting. You may just choose not to, or to be selective as to what you do.

Either way, start assembling 'Team You!', decide and choose

how you're going to account, implement some systems and dive in – regularly. You may surprise yourself and enjoy it!

Happy Accounting!

About Jacqui

After graduating with a Chemistry degree from Imperial College, University of London, Jacqui You qualified as a Chartered Accountant with Arthur Young, now part of EY (formerly Ernst and Young) in the 1980's.

She trained in the Business Services Group (BSG) which provided support and accounting services to entrepreneurs and fledgling businesses who didn't have the financial expertise in house—effectively 'rolling up her shirt sleeves' to work alongside the business owners.

After qualifying, she then spent some time in the training department, where she had the opportunity to mark exam papers for the Institute of Chartered Accountants of England & Wales (ICAEW) which is the governing body for Chartered Accountants in England & Wales.

Jacqui then moved to a start-up retail company which operated in several countries - an exhilarating and challenging time, with lots of 'firefighting', implementing systems and streamlining the Accounts function when turnover increased from £20k to £2m per year almost overnight.

Seeking a new challenge, she joined her father in his Accountancy Practice, 'Norman You Chartered Accountants,' becoming the proprietrix in 1998. She enjoys the diversity of the work and the different ways in which they help, serve and empower their clients – sometimes with their accountancy needs, sometimes in other areas of their lives. . .a truly holistic approach! Many friends and clients refer their children with some clients spanning three generations of the same family.

In 2000, Jacqui spent four months living and travelling in Japan and experimented with being able to manage the Office remotely. Jacqui is also a qualified British Wheel of Yoga teacher and has been involved with Network Marketing since 2007 which introduced her to self-development.

ImpKISS Ltd was created with another Mum from school in 2013 to develop a simple online cashbook. The duo wanted to help more people take away the fear and worry of keeping their accounting records. Their mission is to create a community where people can find knowledge and support from like-minded individuals as they build their businesses. They understand the challenges of developing and growing your business while child rearing, as well as the 'loneliness of the entrepreneur'.

Think of Jacqui and ImpKISS as friends who just happen to have some accountancy knowledge. An 'Imp' is a mythical, magical creature while KISS = Keep It Simple Solutions. Treat them as an extra pair of hands on your team - Team You! – to help support and empower you in your business and life. They want you to look forward to your encounters with them and to leave uplifted with a smile on your face!

You can connect with Jacqui at:
- jacquiyou@gmail.com
- www.twitter.com/@Jacquiyou
- www.linkedin.com/in/jacqui-you

CHAPTER 10

THE SEVEN RESOURCES OF LEADERSHIP

BY JAMES P. NEWTON, Ed.D.

Introduction to the Seven Resources of Leadership

I was in NYS public education for 31 years. I taught for 11 years and was a middle school assistant principal, middle and high school principal and a superintendent for 20 years. I retired July 1, 2017.

However, when I was close to retirement, I started thinking about my teaching days as a technology teacher. One of my favorite lessons to teach was called the seven resources of technology, which was outlined in the NYS technology education curriculum along with a systems approach model for solving problems.

The seven resources of technology are:

1. **People**
2. **Materials**
3. **Tools**
4. **Information**
5. **Energy**
6. **Capital**
7. **Time**

Any technology that exists incorporates the seven resources.

For example:
a) A cell phone needed <u>PEOPLE</u> to develop and design it as well as test the technology.
b) <u>MATERIAL</u> used in the cell phone includes glass, plastic and electronic components.
c) <u>TOOLS</u> were used to assemble the phone.
d) <u>INFORMATION</u> was needed from the engineers and designers and manufacturers who had to have the knowledge to create the cell phone.
e) <u>ENERGY</u> was needed in the forms of human energy, electrical energy, and mechanical energy.
f) The cost or the <u>CAPITAL</u> needed to invest and then produce the cell phone was essential.
g) Finally, the <u>TIME</u> it took to design, build, and then market the cell phone.

All seven resources were used in this technological innovation.

During my two months prior to retirement, I was asked to give a keynote presentation at a banquet for the local Kiwanis club and its annual Youth of the Year banquet. Eight students from two rival local school districts were selected as student leaders of the month. The finale was the annual banquet to select the student of the year from the final eight.

When I was asked to be the keynote speaker for this event, it was apparent that the seven resources of technology would play a key role as I prepared my speech. The Systems approach and the seven resources would be the focus of my speech.

The systems approach is really a great tool since it begins with the goal or the "End in Mind," then it flows into the process, which is where the seven resources come into play. From process is the output, which is the end result. However, there is more to the approach. If the result is not satisfactory after monitoring and evaluating the result, then you go through the process again until you get the expected and desired result.

In the Output of the system you can get four results:

- Unexpected – Undesired
- Unexpected – Desired
- Expected – Undesired
- Expected – Desired

Of course, the goal is to get the Expected and Desired output, however, unexpected and desired can be very rewarding also.

The output is very important, but the process to reach the output is paramount.

A simple example to explain the systems approach is a technological innovation, so I would like to refer back to the cell phone. The goal was to design, build, and market the cell phone. The process was essential as it incorporated the seven resources. The output was the finished product or cell phone. If it was a prototype, more than likely adjustments had to be made and the product went through the systems approach again.

I started thinking about the seven resources of technology and how I have used them in my leadership positions over the years. I had that cathartic moment that hits you. The seven resources easily apply to leadership. So, I wrote my keynote using the seven resources of technology, but incorporated them into the SEVEN RESOURCES OF LEADERSHIP. Below I have listed how I incorporated the seven resources into my leadership presentation:

1. **People** – Interpersonal skills are essential as a leader. In education, you need to work with all stakeholders including parents, students, staff members, and the community. You need to have situational awareness, which means knowing the community that you are leading and being aware of what is going on in the community.

   Michael Fullan, author of the *Six Secrets of Change*, wrote one chapter on Relationships – Relationships – Relationships.

117

It is extremely essential to build relationships with others. Too many times I see the younger generations missing the opportunity to connect face to face because of texting or social media. Put down your phone and talk to someone and build those relationships. That connectedness can be missing at times. I am sure you have witnessed teenagers in a restaurant and they are texting each other instead of talking to one another even though they are sitting next to each other.

People can also have a negative influence on someone, but a leader can address that situation. When I was a middle school principal and high school principal if a student came to me because someone else was bothering him or her I would tell that student – **only you can ruin your day**. No one else can ruin your day. Never let someone ruin your day!

Bullying is a major issue in schools today across the nation. A leader can work with a bullied student or better yet work with the entire school to address this issue. Whether it is cyberbullying or bullying, students can be taught to not be innocent bystanders when they see bullying occur. Students do play a role in bullying situations. Bullies want power and when they have support from other students it increases their power. Students need to learn to not be a supporter of the bully. They need to support the victim. Don't just be an onlooker in a bullying situation. Help the victim and take the power away from the bully.

All students can develop the skills and know how to be leaders against a bully.

Classroom Management - When I was a middle school principal, I was asked to teach a classroom management class for non-tenured teachers. This was a required course. This gave me the opportunity to teach research-based classroom management strategies as well as strategies I have used that, in my humble opinion, worked for me. A teacher is the leader of the classroom, he/she should follow best practices. One of my favorite activities is to pose a question and then have all of my students (teachers in the class) brainstorm. I would use the mind map from Inspiration, a software program.

One example is having teachers focusing on INL's (Intentional Non-Learners). INL's are students who choose not to learn. They have the potential to do well, but choose to not complete assignments or they are tardy and/or absent often. During the brainstorming session we would discuss how a teacher can try to reach or motivate an INL. Some of the responses were, finding something the student is interested in and bringing it into the teacher lesson, or making a connection with student, so once that rapport is established, the student might apply him or herself more in the classroom. Finally, a teacher can have students work in collaborative pairs or small groups, and all students are held accountable for the work, so participation is a must. The classroom management class was great. Teachers shared their management issues with me and we tried to resolve those issues.

2. **Material** – Over the years, we have all learned material through our high school years, college courses and attending workshops and conferences, and reading books. Material can help with the background knowledge necessary to help in your leadership position. One of my favorite material resources was the book titled, *What Great Principals Do Differently*, by Todd Whitaker. He listed fifteen principles that he felt were essential for principals. Three of these principles really stood out to me as a leader:

  (i). It's the people, not programs
  (ii). Treat everyone with respect, everyday, all the time
  (iii). Base every decision on your best teachers

It's the people, not programs – is especially true in schools throughout the nation. Every other year it seems as though new programs are being sold to schools as the answer for increasing student achievement. The company has the data to show the success of the program hoping the school district will spend thousands in purchasing this "amazing" product. When the school decides to purchase and implement the program, they are hopeful that results will be substantial. Yet, if the right person or teacher is not delivering the program, then the program will not be as effective. It is the same with leadership. Without the right person at the helm, a company might not survive. The right person with the right material is essential in a leadership role.

3. **Tools** – We all gather tools in our toolbox over the years and I certainly have. Through our skills and experiences, our tools that we used are sharpened and honed.

Keep Hands To Yourself   Stay To The Right

Newton's No Nonsense Non- Verbal Intervention Program

Walk   Disperse   Stop

Designed By
Courtney Celotto

Mrs. Renee Cool
Teacher of the Hearing Impaired

As an educator, one valuable tool that I used was non-verbal communication. There was a study done by Albert Mehrabian in the 1970's. His study showed that 93% of all communication is non-verbal. 55% is body language and 38% is tone of voice.

I have seen educators escalate or deescalate situations by what they said and how they say it. I am sure all of you remember a teacher who was a screamer. Many times, that teacher would escalate situations, i.e., "Johnny did you leave your brain at home today?" Johnny, if he were a high school student, would probably come back with a "not so nice response" and would probably end up getting suspended for gross insubordination. But the teacher escalated the situation by how he/she communicated with the student.

Non-verbal communication can deescalate a situation. Hand signals or flicking the lights or a soft tone of voice can deescalate a volatile situation. My dissertation was related to non-verbal communication since it reduced low-level violence behaviors in the middle school with non-verbal signals. It showed that low-level violence can be reduced by non-verbal communication. The name of the program is *Newton's No Nonsense Nonverbal Intervention Program (NIP)*. Faculty members used hand signs to deescalate low-level violent behaviors of hitting, kicking, pushing, tripping, and congregating.

Sense of humor is another tool that I use in my leadership position and it can be very effective. When I was a technology teacher, the students used to build bridges out of balsa wood. They designed, built, and destroyed (tested) the bridges. We were checking for the most efficient bridge. The formula was $E = F/W$ which was measured in NEWTONS. When students were building the bridges, I had them use white glue, however, I dyed the glue blue, so I could see how much glue the students were using. The students were not testing the glue, they were testing the design of the bridge. So, I would try to reinforce to them that if you used too much blue glue then it would add weight, which could affect the efficiency formula that is used during the competition. So, I would emphasize to them not to use too much blue glue. Blue glue is good at the right joints, but don't smother the bridge with blue glue.

Morse Code - I am an Amateur Radio Operator and I know the Morse Code. Nowadays that can be seen as not useful. I used to talk to countries all over the world with amateur radio. Even though some people would think Morse Code is obsolete, I still use it. I write messages in yearbooks in Morse Code and students have to look up the messages. People love when I spell their name in Morse Code. As a leader, I introduced students to another language that is considered international:

The Morse Code (.-.. . .- -.. . .-.)

A	.–	J	.---	S	...
B	-...	K	-.-	T	-
C	-.-.	L	.-..	U	..-
D	-..	M	- -	V	...-
E	.	N	-.	W	.--
F	..-.	O	---	X	-..-
G	--.	P	.--.	Y	-.--
H	....	Q	--.-	Z	--..
I	..	R	.-.		

These are a just a few of the tools that I have used in my leadership position.

4. **Information** – Knowledge – Competence – So many people know so much. As a leader you need to be competent in the areas you are leading. In my case I had to be knowledgeable in the areas of teaching, building administration and central office administration. Competence is essential. However, when you are a leader, it is more than just having

information and knowledge about something. President Theodore Roosevelt was quoted as saying, *People do not care how much you know until they know how much you care about them.* People do not care how much you know. They will listen to you and, more than likely, give respect, but did they really connect with you. You need to somehow, someway, connect with the audience or stakeholders you are working with. Knowledge is good, but you also need to show that you care. Caring helped me a great deal in my education profession. Students knew that I cared about them and that helped me to build an exceptional rapport with even the most difficult students. They knew I was knowledgeable about the rules and Code of Conduct, but they also knew I would treat them fairly.

5. **Energy** – Human Energy – WORK ETHIC - LASER
Work Ethic is so important as a leader. If you arrive late and leave early, you as the leader are setting an example. So, more than likely, as the leader, others will follow you. Workers might be happy, but not very productive. You need to have **Light Amplification By Stimulated Emissions of Radiation** (LASER) focus on your goals.

6. **Capital** – Over the years you have invested in yourself. You have paid for your education and you are determined to be a life-long learner. You also need to invest in non-monetary things such as health and nutrition.

7. **Time** – In your leadership role make the most of your time. Be as productive as possible. Time goes by so quickly. My 31 years in public education were a blur.

I would like to end with a quote that refers back to non-verbal communication...

Mother Teresa - Let no one come to you without leaving better and happier. Be the expression of God's kindness in your face, kindness in your eyes, and kindness in your smile. (Non-Verbal)

About Dr. James Newton

Dr. James Preston Newton recently retired after 31 years in public education. He was a technology teacher for 11 years and a public school administrator for 20 years. He served in the roles of middle school assistant principal, middle school principal, high school principal and superintendent in New York State. In 2009, he was named New York State Middle School Principal of the year and was a finalist for the National Middle School Principal of the Year.

As an educator, his focus has always been on improving school climate and increasing student achievement. His doctoral dissertation focused on reducing low-level violent behaviors in the middle school. He developed a program called **N**ewton's No-Nonsense Non-Verbal **I**ntervention **P**rogram to help *NIP* low-level violent behaviors in the bud. He is a certified Olweus Bullying Prevention Trainer and was recently trained as a certified coach, trainer, and speaker.

After retiring, Dr. Newton served as an interim High School principal and he is an Adjunct Professor at Niagara University and St. Bonaventure University. Presently, Dr. Newton has officially come out of retirement to serve as High School Principal in a private school in Buffalo, New York.

Feel free to contact Dr. Newton at:

- jpnewt1@gmail.com.

CHAPTER 11

THE IMPORTANCE OF CULTIVATING A HEALTHY WORK-LIFE BALANCE
FROM A WORKPLACE WELLNESS ADVOCATE

BY NIKKI BUCKSTEAD

It's easy to believe that life coaches have all the answers. However, if there's one thing we realize, it's that life is a journey of discovery. What would be the point in life if we knew each expected outcome? Life coaches impart tools, techniques and practices to find fulfillment, balance and happiness in the midst of life's surprises.

I came into this line of work from one of a polar opposite. In fact, in 2006, the 36-year-old me, an ambitious and driven CEO, would be quite puzzled that I "gave it all up" to meditate and practice yoga all day! But of course, that's not what I really do and it's not as simple as that. Much of what attracted me to this line of work was my own critical mass: many successes and many facets of business life, including wealth and stress. But something greater was calling me that I could no longer ignore. And that calling was to inspire and empower people to find their own balance and happiness. And that has brought about a much deeper sense of contentment, balance and happiness than I found in the busy hustle of my career.

My focus now is on life coaching and workplace wellness. Having worked in behavioral health for over 20+ years, I found it ironic that as much as we were working to help others overcome unhealthy behaviors, we were not always taking our own advice. Stress, anxiety, and fatigue seemed to be par for the course. Now, I get to work with individuals and companies to help them discover what inspires them, brings them joy and learn to live their lives with purpose and passion. I work with businesses to help create healthy workplace models that decrease stress, burnout and compassion fatigue, while increasing employee satisfaction on the job.

Only with the right combination of self-care, support and guidance from professionals like counselors, mentors, life coaches, therapists and spiritual teachers, can we begin to unravel the self-limiting beliefs, self-sabotaging behavior and reconnect to our higher self. One where we begin the journey to healing, self-discovery and following our passion.

Self-care is an going event in our lives and differs from day to day. Self-care isn't the same as spending a day at the spa getting a facial and mani/pedi. And while days like that are amazing, they don't cultivate the necessary reliance that is needed to manage our daily lives and appropriately handle stress and turmoil. Some days we will only have a few moments to practice self-care, so it's important to set up a routine and an acknowledgment that you are worthy of taking the time for yourself. This Chapter sets out to help support you in your busy lives, live your best life and prioritize wellness and mental health in a few easy-to-maintain ways.

UNPLUG

If only we would have known how much control our smart devices would soon take over our brain and time! Finding and prioritizing time to unplug is the one of the key ways to see improvements in our overall wellness and well-being. But "unplugging" can also be a metaphor for our connection to things that no longer serve our highest self, and how important it can be to analyze and renegotiate that time and connection for things that do serve us. Smart phones were designed to keep us connected, however research shows a dramatic increase in Americans feeling more alone and isolated than ever.

The good news is, to change this behavior is in our control and doesn't take very long. It doesn't mean it's easy, if you find yourself disconnected from life or using social media or binge watching too much, you will find that changing one behavior may help you feel more connected and engaged with life. When we seek to reduce our screen time, we find we can connect more easily with others and ourselves. This allows the space for us to find ways to be more present in our daily lives.

These days, work-life balance can seem like an impossible feat. With so many competing demands on our time plus technology makes working accessible around the clock. And with the advent of a computer in your pocket, our smartphones have made it easier for us to stay connected long after we have left the office.

Ultimately, it is up to us to set the priorities. A few ways to unplug:

- Consider not sending those texts at your kid's soccer game or not sending work emails while you're with your family or friends. Make quality time true quality time.
- Find set times every day (especially on weekends) to turn the phone on silent or do not disturb. Your phone has settings that allow important or "emergency calls" to come through but turn off other things like email, Instagram and Facebook comments.

- Consider finding activities with your friends and loved ones, or alone that require your phone being turned off: going to the movies, hiking, gardening, etc.

- Leave notes for your family or loved ones instead of texts. Buy birthday and other celebratory cards in lieu of online cards. It's something that can be cherished for years to come.

REFRAME NEGATIVE THOUGHTS

Reframing is an important strategy to keep your mind healthy and continue to look for the positive in your circumstances. Self-limiting beliefs are the number one thing I help my clients with. These beliefs stem from years, if not decades of self-doubt and low self-worth that has crept in and taken up free rent in our minds. These beliefs are ideas that were told to us by our parents, siblings, teachers, friends, bosses, and spouses, etc. They are words that we have come to believe as the truth – our truth. And they hold us back from becoming who we want be. Research shows we have between 60,000-80,000 thoughts per day and 90% of those thoughts we had the day before. So we continue to tell ourselves the same story over and over again – even if it was never true to begin with!

I work with my clients on learning to identify and trust their inner guide, gut instinct, intuition – whatever you want to call it. There are ways to begin to cultivate trusting your intuition, but it does take some practice. I think we have all had an experience, or several experiences where we knew something was off, but couldn't put our finger on it. Or where we got this feeling in our gut to take a different route, rather than the street or parking lot that looked empty and dark.

So much of our self-limiting beliefs come from fear. Mostly, fear of failure. But this perceived failure creates stress and anxiety, and sometimes we actually become paralyzed with fear. Perceived failure robs us of our self-worth – which in turn creates many problems, including self-sabotaging behaviors. We begin to underestimate ourselves, criticizing and judging ourselves, sometimes harshly. We stop taking healthy risks and take the "safe route."

To counter the effects of perceived failure, it is pertinent we look at the whole picture, not just the end result. I always ask myself:

— "What did I learn about myself in this situation?"
— "Was there a time I didn't trust my gut instinct?"
— "If I am faced with this situation again, what can I do differently?"

In my experience, one thing I can always point back to when something has failed was not following my gut instinct. And for me, there was a direct correlation to stress and anxiety when not following my intuition.

Negative self-talk tricks us. We don't even hear ourselves think it anymore. Sometimes it's so quiet it's like a whisper. Other times it's so loud, it's all we can hear:

"You can't."

"You're not _____ enough."

Fill in the blank…Smart…Good…Pretty…Tall. . .Lucky…Young …Thin…Talented. Whatever it is, start to notice what you are saying to yourself. And when you hear that happen, acknowledge it, and replace it with a new, healthy thought about yourself.

"The truth is, I am good enough…"

Changing old thought patterns isn't always easy, but it is a way to a new freedom and a way to begin living your life in a meaningful way – free of self-doubt and self-sabotaging behaviors. Working with a life coach or other trusted professional on this issue is one way to help you see when the pattern creeps up, and can help you develop a new, healthy thought pattern.

Thoughts in the brain are like walking through a grassy field. Each time you have the same thought, it creates a groove in the brain – which makes it that much easier for the thought to come up and travel down the same groove again. When walking through a grassy field, taking the same path day after day creates an easy pathway. The grass is flat and you can see where you are going. The brain acts in the same way. The good news is that you can change that. This phenomenon in the brain is called neuroplasticity, and new research is coming out every day to support that we can, in fact, change the brain's ability to reorganize itself, by forming new neural connections throughout life which allows the neurons to adjust their activities in response to new situations or to changes in their environment.

<u>NATURE HEALS</u>

Science has found substantial evidence that being in nature can help fight chronic diseases, relieve stress and depression, promote faster healing, stronger immune systems, and more. And new research is beginning to reveal why: connecting with nature affects us, mentally and physically, right down to our cells.

A Stanford study looked at the brains of volunteers who either walked in a field of oak trees or along a busy road. No change was observed in the urban walkers, but the nature walkers had suppressed activity in a region of the brain associated with rumination, which frequently occurs with depression.

Having worked in this field over many years, "being in nature" was often a prescription for depression and anxiety. You may have noticed that after you spend time in the outdoors, you come back happier, less stressed, revitalized and more focused. A growing body of research is finding there's a measurable difference when we perform activities out in nature versus indoors.

A recent Australian and UK study also found that people who visited parks for 30 minutes or more each week were much less likely to have high blood pressure than those who didn't. Several studies have shown that adults who exercised in nature had lower levels of tension, confusion, anger and depression than when they exercised indoors.

But why? Some of the effects appear to be psychological in origin. Natural scenes and activities can stimulate our sense of wonder, making our concerns seem less significant, while stimulating the feeling that we're part of something larger than ourselves. This can measurably reduce stress, anxiety and depression.

Three Easy Ways to Get Into Nature:

1. Set recurring reminders on your work calendar, just 15 minutes a day, to go outside. This will break up the pattern of your day, get your blood circulating, and be a healthy habit.

2. Working out a complex problem? Walk on it. Anytime you find yourself struggling to compose an email, break down a concept for a presentation, or even blocked thinking on a new idea, take yourself outside to sort it out. You'll come back refreshed and ready to dive back in.

3. Make plans that involve the outdoors. On your nights and weekends with family and friends, find ways to spend more time in nature. This can be as simple as bringing a picnic to the park or trying a new trail system when you walk your dog.

MOVE AND MEDITATE

Even when we're busy, we make time for the crucial things in life. We eat. We go to the bathroom. We sleep. And yet our most crucial needs are often the first thing to go when our calendars fill up. There are two incredibly (and free) stress reducers and brain activators out there, and you're probably not doing them.

- Exercise
- Meditation

Exercise is an effective stress reducer. It pumps feel-good endorphins through your body. Equally beneficial, and equally discarded when life plans fill up, meditation is the antidote to stress.

As a meditation teacher, one of the things I teach my class is about what happens in your body when you experience a stressful situation. We have grown so disconnected from our bodies that we can't even identify when we are going through a stressful response. When we experience stress, our brains and bodies go into "Fight or Flight." This happens when we experience a perceived harmful attack or threat to our survival. The part of our brain that controls this, the **amygdala**, is the one part of our brain that hasn't evolved since the caveman days. So, regardless of whether we were cut off on the freeway, or a saber-tooth tiger is going to attack us, our brain perceives the threat in the same way. Research also shows that we experience this fight or flight scenario five to seven times per day, and it takes 20-60 minutes for our bodies and brain to return back to homeostasis. That means we are potentially in this state for up to seven hours per day! And we wonder why we are so fatigued!

When I ask people why they come to me, some reply that it's to learn about meditation and many tell me their doctors recommended it. Even healthcare providers know meditation offers something that no prescription medication can.

Not-so-fun fact: Approximately 40 million American adults suffer from anxiety (those who have identified and reported it). Millions more may not even have the language or context to understand how they are feeling. Many of the Workplace Wellness programs I have administered include meditation programs, including classes on learning how to meditate and how to have an ongoing at-home practice as part of a self-care routine.

Meditation can feel daunting to some people. So start small! Again, just five minutes in the morning and night can combat sleep issues, decrease stress hormones, as well as just bringing us back to even state. And it increases calmness and happiness. Who doesn't want that?

Exercises can require minor effort but offer major payoffs. Exercise increases the feel-good hormones, releases stress, helps us sleep better and of course, feel better. Exercise doesn't have to be an hour at the gym, it can be a 20-minute walk with your kids, 15 minutes of chair yoga at your office, stretching, etc. Consider taking the stairs instead of the elevator or choose a parking spot further away. Every day doesn't have to be a major, sweaty workout. But get moving. Remember…if you rest, you rust.

IN CLOSING

Work-life balance means something different to every individual. There comes a price with our culture of always being available and "on": we're slowly killing ourselves. Experts agree: the compounding stress from the never-ending workday is damaging. It can hurt relationships, health, and overall happiness.

That's why it's up to us to cultivate our own self-care. We must implement good intentions that free us up to do demanding work and get the most out of our personal lives. This chapter has outlined several methods that, in combination, give a terrific foundation for self-care and wellness. Implementing these practices will take a little adjustment but over time, you will see great rewards.

To dive deeper into wellness, ask your HR or workplace manager if they have a budget to bring in a wellness specialist quarterly. Or consider visiting your own life coach to find deeper ways to integrate these healing practices into your daily life.

Meditation, releasing self-limiting beliefs/self-sabotage, finding a tribe or community, having your own hobby/time to yourself, recognizing how stress, burnout and compassion fatigue the body and spending time in nature are all meaningful ways to do this.

Beginning a regular self-care routine is critical to being our best. I often use this example: when on an airplane, the flight attendant always says, "Should the cabin pressure change, put on your own oxygen mask first, then assist another." There is a reason for this. If you aren't caring for yourself first, you are unable to give to others in a healthy way.

About Nikki

Nikki Buckstead is passionate about empowering people to find their truth and purpose in life. As the Founder and Owner of Transformative Coaching & Consulting Services in Orange County, California, Nikki successfully serves clients going through various life transitions and challenges.

Nikki's central gift to the world is helping other people find their unique talents so that they can become architects of their own lives. She focuses on helping others find clarity and live with passion and purpose. Whether it is through guided meditation, corporate training, or one-on-one coaching, Nikki serves the mind, body and spirit in personal and professional growth that helps her clients achieve positive, lasting results. Nikki provides a safe, supportive, and sacred space to connect with her clients, which makes them feel inspired, and helps them to create the life they desire.

For nearly 25 years, Nikki has worked or volunteered in the nonprofit sector, been an executive in behavioral health, and has served as a leader and advocate in multiple nonprofit organizations. With each cause she has been a part of, Nikki has brought a deep passion to her work, and has always focused on helping others succeed.

In 2000, Nikki began working for the National Council on Alcoholism and Drug Dependence (NCADD) – Sacramento Region Affiliate – and soon after became the CEO. Her executive experience at such a young age taught her the hard-way, the importance of self-care, avoiding burnout and maintaining a healthy work-life balance. After leaving in 2011, Nikki continued her work in the nonprofit, behavioral health field for several more years before founding Transformative Coaching and Consulting Services.

Currently, Nikki also serves as the President of the Holistic Chamber of Commerce of Huntington Beach. When she is not serving on a national board of a nonprofit, or coaching executives in holistic wellbeing, Nikki loves to travel. Most recently, she has visited Cambodia and Vietnam on a solo journey. She also enjoys being in nature, especially near coastal regions. Although Nikki currently lives in Southern California, she has previously lived in various parts of the United States, calling Sacramento her home for most of those years.

Nikki practices daily meditation and yoga and is Certified in Meditation and Ayurveda through the Chopra Center. Nikki teaches classes on goal setting, personal meditation, identifying and releasing limiting beliefs and self-sabotaging behaviors as well as radical self-care workshops, among many others. Nikki is also a certified Yoga instructor.

Importantly to Nikki as well, is the fact that she has been in recovery for over 30 continuous years. Nikki believes that her sobriety has been the humble, formidable spiritual foundation to make all of the good in her life possible. With her vast expertise, holistic delivery, scheduled accountability, and speed of results, Nikki can empower you to become Your Best Self!

Nikki has a Master's degree in Psychology and has also served as Executive Director for the National Alliance on Mental Illness (NAMI), Sonoma County. She has worked as a consultant for Substance Abuse and Mental Health Services Administration, the National Wellness Institute, and the She Recovers Foundation. She also holds certification in Workplace Wellness Management.

You can connect with Nikki:

- Online: https://www.nikkibuckstead.com
- Email: coaching@nikkibuckstead.com
- Phone: (714) 880-4134
- LinkedIn: Nikki Buckstead

CHAPTER 12

YOUR HOME – YOUR FUTURE WEALTH CREATOR

BY BARBARA & SEYCHELLE VAN POOLE

Did you know that choosing where you and your family live could be one of the most important decisions you make for creating wealth for you and your family? A home is usually your largest investment and could be your greatest wealth determiner, if selected wisely. In addition, deciding to invest in rental properties can significantly increase your wealth even more.

As a team, we have helped over 2,200 families buy and sell homes. Our passion is helping people, and we want to help as many people as we can. As Realtors®, we are blessed to be able to help people with buying and selling their family homes and building wealth through real estate. We realized that to help more people, we needed to build a strong team of professional Realtors® who would have this same passion for helping people. We have been blessed to attract a talented group of Realtors® who truly care about consulting our clients through this important decision-making process.

According to Maslow's hierarchy of needs, a home and a place to live is a basic human need. Moving and changing where you live can be a major life stressor. And moving usually comes with some other major life stress, as well. When people decide to move, it is usually because of some other significant life event like a birth, a death, a marriage, a divorce, loss of a job, a career change or job transfer, a health issue, children moving in or out of the home, or parents moving into the home. As Realtors®, we are honored to have a positive impact during a crucial time in their lives.

Making informed decisions about your real estate needs will help ensure your financial success. Hiring the best professionals to direct you through this real estate process is crucial, so here are important guidelines to assist you in creating your optimal outcome.

Decision 1: Buy or Rent? Purchase Investment Properties?

Deciding whether to buy or rent a home could make a huge difference in your family's wealth. According to the Federal Reserve's Survey of Consumer Finances in the United States in 2016, the median family wealth of a renter was $5,200. Contrast that number with the median family wealth of a home owner of $231,400. This means that the median family net worth of a home owner is almost 45 times greater than a renter's family median net worth.

One of our clients, Alicia, had always rented. She decided that she wanted to own a home. Alicia had very good credit. However, like most renters, she had accumulated only $3,000 in savings. She asked her mother if she would help her with the down payment. They reached an agreement that her mother would gift the down payment to her and, when Alicia sold her home, Alicia would gift the same amount back to her mother, and then she and her mother would split any profits. Approximately 18 months after the purchase of her home, Alicia's job was transferred to another city. Alicia sold her home, and she and her mother profited over

$30,000 which earned them each $15,000 in only 18 months. If Alicia had instead continued to rent, she would still only have $3,000 in savings instead of $15,000.

By purchasing a home, you are building your future wealth. When you are renting a home or apartment, you are building someone else's wealth by paying their mortgage payments for them. This is why investing in additional residential real estate to lease to others is such a good investment.

When purchasing a home for your personal residence, you can usually borrow 80-100% of the money needed to purchase a home. When purchasing a rental home, you can often borrow 80% of the money needed to purchase the home. For most other types of investments like stocks, you have to come up with 100% of the money, instead of the 20% needed to buy a rental property. When you lease the home, your tenant pays you rent which you can use to pay for your mortgage loan, repairs, taxes and insurance. This means that you will gain 100% of the value over time plus any appreciation on the home value. And remember that you only invested 20% of the original value of the home.

John, another client, owned a home that had $100,000 in home equity. He took out a home equity loan and then started buying investment homes which he leased to families. With 20% down on each property, he used his $100,000 as down payments and purchased $500,000 in rental properties.

Over the next ten years, John's rentals appreciated in value to be worth $1,200,000. He also paid off the bulk of his loans and only owed $120,000 on his properties. After selling his properties, he had turned his $100,000 into a $1,000,000 net worth. That means he had a 100% return on his money each year for 10 years. With stocks averaging 7-12% returns, you would have to have the same money invested for 142 years to get the same profit in the stock market.

As you can see, owning your own home and then investing in homes to lease can substantially increase your wealth. To have the best chance of success, you will need to hire a Realtor® to be your consultant for making these important decisions.

We were introduced to Thomas after he had attempted to sell his property himself. He had a $400,000 home on the market and it took him nine months to find a buyer by having his home as a "For Sale By Owner." He then got a contract, the buyer stalled for another three months, and then the buyer decided not to buy the house. With over 75% of real estate law suits involving one side representing themselves, Thomas found himself suing the buyer for non-performance, but did not win his lawsuit. After $25,000 in legal fees and over one year of chasing the buyer, Thomas asked us to sell his home. If we had worked with Thomas from the beginning, we would have saved him a year of frustration and over $25,000 in legal fees. In addition, we sold his home for $425,000 instead of the $400,000 he was originally asking.

Obviously, you wouldn't think of performing surgery on yourself if you needed surgery, so why would you want to make your important real estate decisions without the best professional Realtor® advising you?

Decision 2: How do you find the best Realtor®?

Since your home purchase is such an important decision, selecting the best professional to assist you is a significant determiner of your success.

HOW TO HIRE A PROFESSIONAL REALTOR®

Criteria 1: Team vs Individual Agent: Are they an individual agent or are they part of a team? Depending on the structure of the real estate team, having a team of Realtors® working on your behalf could provide you with more expertise on the home market and better negotiating skills. A team could also have more agents available to show you homes and to respond to your questions and needs in a timely manner.

Criteria 2: Experience: What is their experience and what is their record of success? You will want to find out how many homes they have sold, or how many homes they sell each year. Surprisingly, many Realtors® only sell 3-5 homes per year. Hiring someone who sells well above this number each year means they see more homes and trends faster – which can benefit you as the customer.

Criteria 3: Market Knowledge: To evaluate their market knowledge, you will want to ask how many homes they have sold in your preferred area and neighborhoods. Are they aware of "off market" properties? Are they part of a network of Realtors® who keep each other informed on upcoming real estate trends? Obviously, the more knowledgeable they are about the real estate market and trends in your desired area, the higher your chances of success.

Criteria 4: Negotiating Techniques: What negotiating techniques do they use to help you "win" in a multiple offer situation? How strong are their negotiating skills? Their number of successful sales is a strong indicator of their negotiating effectiveness. Remember that the goal is a successful transaction that meets both parties' needs. If either party feels that they are being "taken advantage of", they will find a way out of the deal.

Criteria 5: Client Satisfaction and Reputation: How do their past clients rate their performance and what do their client testimonials say? What awards have they won? How does their performance compare with other Realtors®? How comfortable are you with their integrity, communication skills, and attentiveness to your needs?

Criteria 6: Investment Property Experience & Resources: If you have decided to invest in additional homes to lease, then you will want to be sure that the Realtor® you select has experience in investment properties. Do they have experience evaluating investment properties? Does your Realtor® successfully invest in real estate? Do they work with investors? Are they an expert at analyzing the rental market? Do they list properties for lease? Do they have a network of resources to assist you with any necessary renovations, repairs, and tenant and property management?

For a rental property, you want to be sure the property analysis meets the following criteria:

- The neighborhood is attractive to tenants – safe, good schools (if attracting families is a priority), accessible, near amenities like shopping, restaurants, and local activities.

- Average lease rates for similar properties will ideally cover your loan payments (principal and interest), taxes, insurance, some maintenance, and property management fees plus profit.

- Average time to lease similar properties is short, so your property leases quickly.

- The neighborhood is appreciating in value. Has the property historically gone up in value over time and will it likely increase in the future? If there is currently an economic downturn, look at the historic trends and the best projection for the future after the economic recovery. An economic downturn can be a great time to buy properties at a lower cost, but then the analysis is even more important to predict future performance.

If you also have a home you need to sell, you need the following information:

Criteria 7: Home Sales Success Record: How many homes have they sold in the past year? What is their system for generating multiple offers? What percentage of the homes that they sell receive multiple offers? What is their average Sales Price to List Price percentage? What is their average time on market to sell a home? How does their success record compare with other Realtors®?

Criteria 8: Marketing Plan: Most Realtors® do what they call the 3 P's of Real Estate. They PUT a sign in the yard, PUT the home on MLS, and then PRAY that the home sells. Instead, you need a marketing expert. Their Marketing Plan is very important for getting your home sold for the most money in the shortest amount of time with the least hassle. How will they successfully market your home to the most buyers? How many websites will feature your home? Are they part of any referral or relocation networks? How do they expose your home to local, national, and international buyers? How often will they bring motivated buyers to your home?

Criteria 9: Home Preparation Services: Do they provide a stager to consult with you on preparing your home to appeal to the most buyers? Do they use a professional photographer for home photographs? Do they provide extras like virtual floor plans, aerial photographs, or auction services? What other services do they offer?

Criteria 10: Resources: You are entitled to additional benefits. Are they handling the coordination to be sure that your transaction closes and funds smoothly? Currently, our closing checklist has over 120 steps to be completed after a home is under contract. Are they coordinating with the lenders, title companies, real estate attorneys, surveyors, appraisers, and other Realtors®? Do they have a list of competent resources like home warranty companies, insurance companies, lenders, contractors, plumbers, electricians, painters, heating and air conditioning companies, fencing companies, and movers to recommend? Do they offer a concierge service?

In conclusion, by systematically gathering and analyzing the above information, you can make an informed decision and select the best Realtor® to assist you. Working together, you can make your real estate dreams come true, find a great home for you and your family, and keep yourself on track to build generational wealth for you and your family.

About Barbara & Seychelle

Barbara Van Poole is the Founder and Seychelle Van Poole is the Team Director of the Van Poole Properties Group at Keller Williams Realty. Their real estate group has helped over 2,200 families successfully buy and sell homes, which puts them in the top 1% of real estate professionals in the United States. They currently sell homes throughout the Dallas – Fort Worth and Austin areas and are continuing their expansion growth into additional cities.

As sought-after national speakers, presenters, and teachers, Barbara and Seychelle have been featured as Real Estate experts on ABC, CBS, HGTV, Fox News, Dallas Morning News, and America Tonight. Barbara, Seychelle, and their company have repeatedly been named the "Best Realtors" by *D Magazine* and *Texas Monthly.*

Barbara is a Real Estate Broker Associate, Realtor®, Certified Real Estate Specialist (CRS), Accredited Buyer Representative (ABR), Graduate Realtor Institute (GRI), International Real Estate Specialist (IRES), and Keller Williams International Luxury Specialist.

Barbara earned a degree in marketing and taught at the College of Business at the University of Texas in Austin as a Ph.D. candidate. She then consulted with major corporations on new product development. After backpacking around the world studying cultures, Barbara did post graduate studies in interior design. She then managed a commercial interior design company and developed commercial real estate. In 2001, Barbara started the Van Poole Properties Group. She and her team have built Van Poole Properties Group to be one of the highest producing Real Estate teams internationally.

Seychelle Van Poole Engelhard is Barbara's daughter. She joined Van Poole Properties Group in 2004 after working for a global advertising agency in New York. Seychelle was named to "Top 30 Realtors Under 30" by the National Association of Realtors and awarded the "Regional Impact Award" by Keller Williams International. She is a Broker Associate and Realtor®.

The Van Pooles are passionate about helping people build wealth through

Real Estate. They believe that the home buying, selling, and investing decision is an important one, and this decision makes a true difference in people's wealth, lifestyle, and quality of life. By providing the best advice and service to their clients on their home decisions, their team has successfully created raving fans. They understand that buying, selling, and moving can be a stressful time, and their goal is to provide their clients with the best information to make great Real Estate decisions for their families. They believe that it is an honor to be able to help people during this pivotal time.

In addition, Barbara, Seychelle, and their leadership team have carefully selected and trained a team of professional Realtors® who also thrive by helping people. They are passionate about creating opportunities and developing successful careers in Real Estate by helping their clients reach their goals. When you help enough people achieve their dreams, your own dreams will also come true.

Contact Barbara and Seychelle Van Poole and their Real Estate team of professionals at:

- Van Poole Properties Group, Keller Williams Realty
- Tel: 972-608-0777
- Email: Info@VanPoole.com
- Website: www.VanPooleProperties.com

CHAPTER 13

BUTTERFLIES

BY CHARLOTTE BENZ

Clutching my newborn baby boy, I could feel my heart thumping my chest so vigorously that I thought it'd wake him. I took a deep breath and gently touched his delicate face. I glanced up then at my beautiful little girl, still only a toddler; precious and innocent.

The world outside passed by as the train led us to new unfamiliar horizons. The world within me, my world, had come to an end. This was the day my old life had reached its disturbing crescendo and expired.

I had pretended to be happy so convincingly, that I had even fooled myself. I realise now that Life is never fooled, it listens to even the faintest murmur of desire. And the core of me deeply desired a profound life.

So, in response to my heart's desire, I was shaken awake; the spell of denial I'd put over myself, was smashed. Suddenly, I saw it all, as it truly was – the truth, with its jagged and dangerous edges. In the midst of the fresh and consuming pain, I couldn't perceive it as yet, but this was the beginning of my prayers being answered.

With my toddler and newborn, I had escaped a destructive

relationship. I arrived on the Isle of Wight as a newly single and traumatised mother. More frightening drama was to follow, and I was put on police protection. Living out of a suitcase, struggling to make ends meet with my children in tow and always looking over my shoulder, this situation was more than just challenging.

In the midst of it all, I would receive these intuitive nudges to allow time for myself so I could re-energise. In particular, I'd have the repeated insight to do a practice called Emotional Freedom Technique or 'Tapping'. Despite the fact that I had done Tapping before, with incredible results, and was even trained as a practitioner, I repeatedly told myself there was no time for me, that the kids needs came first.

In truth, whenever thoughts of any effective healing tool came to me, such as prayer, meditation, being in nature or using pure essential oils... the fearful part of me allowed the long list of daily 'to do's' take priority. Another day would pass and once more, I was left depleted.

Life was like a violent ebb and flow of sea. Mostly, it felt like I could just about keep above the water. But then those horrible moments of overwhelm would wash over me, like a great wave of negativity, so that I thought I was literally going to drown. I'd feel so many emotions... hopelessness, guilt and anxiety. I felt LIFE had let me down.

I recall how I looked in on my babies sleeping one evening, saw how beautiful and peaceful they were. Overwhelmed with emotion suddenly, I started to cry. Big, fat, sorrowful tears that felt like sobs of the soul. I was my children's role model, their source of love and protection, their everything, and I was playing small and powerless.

I knew in my heart I had the power to shift my perception and look for the gift in this situation. I could embrace the new life I found myself in as opportunity to learn and grow, or I could break down and leave my children with no mother.

That is when I surrendered.

Dearest Divine, please give me the courage to trust in Life. I need your strength and love so I can be the best mother to my children. I do believe that everything happens for our highest good, that there has to be something incredible to come out of all of this, so please show me the gift. I am ready now.

I closed my eyes and focused on my breath. As I inhaled I imagined breathing in peace and white light and as I exhaled I imagined letting go of all my worries. Then, as if gently guided by an unknown energy of Love, I listened at last, to that inner voice and began to Tap.

I allowed my hand to move intuitively from one meridian point to another on my body. As I tapped each meridian, I spoke out loud, all I felt in that moment. More and more words came; the disempowering stories I'd been telling myself for years, the hurt feelings I'd buried deep. I let it all out and my face, hands and chest were sodden with tears. As I continued to express my truth, the warmth of new-found determination was awakening in me. And then it was reassuring words of hope, truth and positivity that fell from my lips.

When I had voiced it all, I stopped, took a deep, grounding breath and placed my hands on my heart. Sitting in the silent light of the moon, I knew something profound had happened. This first tapping felt like a relief and a victory.

New-found gratitude rose from my soul and I gave thanks for this moment. I thanked the Moon for shining on my children and me. I thanked my heart for pumping life through my veins. It all made sense now and I felt joy for my life, for my children, of all that had been and all that would be.

THE RECIPE FOR SUCCESS

I awoke early the next morning, brimming with enthusiasm and together with my children went on an adventure. We collected Nature's treasures, danced barefoot on the sand and we shared endless cuddles. I was blessed to be living on the coast of the magical Isle of Wight, and only from that moment did I see what a gift it was. I could now appreciate the sweetness of the sea air in my chest and the warmth of the breeze through my hair. Being mentally present, in the midst of Nature, with my laughing children, was exquisite.

Nothing in my situation had shifted. But life suddenly was so precious to me. Why? Because I had chosen to think another thought. So simple. Instead of resisting what was, I now said Yes! And for the first time in a long time. . . I was happy.

Being in Nature with my children became a daily pleasure and I was left feeling both rejuvenated and earthed. I started diffusing dōTERRA Certified Pure Therapeutic Grade essential oils and found specific emotion blends, such as Console, Serenity and Elevation, both comforting and uplifting. Whenever I found a pocket of time in the day, I would tap and each time it felt like a mini gift to myself. Every short routine got me a little bit further along my journey of recovery.

I now noticed a lightness in my step and would catch myself singing. I kept seeing butterflies; spiritual confirmation of being in Life's flow. More faith filled, I listened to messages from my Higher Self and as a result, not only did my business begin to thrive, but I now knew my Life purpose and started making intentions and working on goals in alignment with it.

You too can live an inspired creative life!

When we are hurting; in the midst of our life-changing event, it can feel like it will never end. This isn't true; have Faith that this too will pass. No storm lasts forever.

I am delighted to share with you eleven healing tools that were both my saviour and metamorphosis. I call them Butterflies. Take the time to embrace any of the Butterflies and they will help you on your transformational journey.

1. Allow Yourself to Grieve
   When going through your challenge, it is important you give yourself the time to release any negative emotions. It is part of being human and part of the healing process. By putting on a 'brave face' or distracting yourself from feeling, those negative energies stay with you. This prolongs the journey of recovery. Give yourself permission to cry those big fat tears and let it all out, guilt free!

   Another tool for getting all our mental and emotional 'gunk' out, is to journal. Wake every morning and write whatever comes into your mind. You'll be astounded by the creative insights that occur when the mind is cleared.

2. You Are Not Alone
   You are a human being and part of the human experience is challenge. No one escapes adversity, no matter how successful or spiritual. Rest assured you are not alone in your pain; there are plenty of people going through their own dramas. Life will never give you more than you can handle, ever.

3. Keep Your Vibration High
   When going through your troubling time, it is imperative you do all you can to keep a positive perspective. Firstly, I recommend you keep company with people who make you feel good, who genuinely love and support you. Now is not the time for lectures and judgements, this will only bring you down further.

   Read books and watch movies that delight and inspire you. Replace watching and reading the news with enlightening music or motivational programmes.

4. Surrender

If you want to stop your suffering, then simply surrender to your situation. Whatever you are going through, no amount of complaints, blaming, shaming or shouting is going to change a thing. In fact, this creates more stress and as a result we ultimately suffer. Yes, suffering is optional. Imagine swimming upstream, against the river's current. It is exhausting and gets you nowhere fast. This is how resistance feels. Now imagine floating downstream carried by the river's flow. This is how surrender feels.

All you have gone through or are going through is part of the plan, a beautiful, perfect plan. All you have to do is say "Yes" to the new and unfamiliar. The past is in the past; let it go. The best is yet to come; have faith.

5. Connect with Nature

Nature is healing. Getting out and connecting with nature as often as you can, is rejuvenating and brings peace. Walking barefoot on sand or soil grounds us; literally connecting us to the Earth's energetic flow. It harmonises the body, resulting in deep emotional, physical and mental well-being.

6. Give to Yourself

Often, during the hardest times in our lives, we can neglect ourselves when ironically, we need the self-love and nourishment the most. It is not selfish nor is it irresponsible to care for yourself. It is never at the expense of others, quite the contrary; when you regularly give to yourself, your energy levels are higher, your mind is clearer, and you radiate peace. When you fill your metaphoric well with vitality and love, the overflow of good energy can be generously shared with your loved ones.

Go on a date with yourself every week. That means no children, friends or significant others, just you. Do what you truly enjoy; something that excites the inner child in you. This is your sacred time, schedule it and allow nothing else to take priority. You'll feel renewed and your tolerance levels will rise.

7. Eat Healthily and Supplement
Eating a nutritious and balanced diet is the foundation of our health and is particularly important when under stress. What we eat affects our energy levels and our mood, so eating right can make all the difference to our physical and mental vitality and stress levels. It can be tempting to choose unhealthy foods as quick emotional fixes and for convenience, but long term we are left depleted. Plan nutritious meals whenever you can. Preferably go organic, which also reduces chemicals and other toxins from your diet.

I also recommend adding a daily supplement designed to help promote energy, health, and vitality. I use dōTERRA's Lifelong Vitality supplement which is full of essential nutrients, metabolism benefits, and powerful antioxidants

8. Use CPTG Essential Oils
Having dōTERRA Certified Pure Therapeutic Grade (CPTG) essential oils as a major part of my health and wellness regime is a true gift to me and my children. During times of stress, our immune system can weaken, so it is vital to boost immunity to prevent illness. dōTERRA essential oils do just that. They are Nature's medicine; having all the medicinal benefits without any of the negative side effects. Essential oils also help improve mood, energy and focus. Using specific emotional oil blends during healing practices, such as Tapping, can even make the practice more powerful.

Diffuse essential oils throughout the day, at home or work, to elevate your mood or help relax you. Also, during moments of high stress, simply inhale from the bottle or apply a drop of oil onto your heart and reflex points.

9. Forgive

When we feel aggrieved, we often project resentment or anger onto the offending person or situation. By pointing the finger, we assume the 'wrong-doer' is in some way being punished. The truth, however, is that the only one suffering is you, as this quote puts it:

"Resentment is like drinking poison and waiting for the other person to die."

Remember, it's not what happened to you that evoked these negative feelings, but your thought about it. In truth, no one has the power to make you feel anything. It's our judgement that creates the feeling. Therefore, instead of giving your power away; stick to the true facts and think a thought that empowers you.

A great way to help you forgive is to look for the lesson and the blessing in your challenging situation. Yes, every cloud has a silver lining.

10. Tapping for Emotional Freedom

Tapping is a powerful healing tool that allows us to let go of trauma and other negative emotions in minutes. Simply by tapping the meridians of your body with your fingertips and vocalising traumatic memories, the brain, energy system and body simultaneously alter, restoring our being to a harmonious state.

Tapping is fast and so easy to learn and do. You can tap on anything, including anxiety, phobias, trauma, forgiveness and physical pain. Whatever you are going through, you can heal it with Tapping. Yes, it's that powerful!

11. Gratitude

The more we see the good in our lives and give thanks for it, the more good stuff will show up for us to appreciate.

Gratitude raises our vibration and when our vibes are high, we attract things that also vibrate at that same frequency. The same is true when our vibes are low; like attracts like. This is called the Law of Attraction and it is a spiritual law as real as gravity. We want to do all we can to raise ourselves up and gratitude is a sure-fire way to do this. So ask yourself, what have I got in my life right now that I am grateful for? And yes, you have so many wonderful blessings in your life. Count them all!

About Charlotte

Charlotte Benz is the mother of two children who inspire her every day. Together they live in beautiful Southern Ireland. Charlotte is a committed Wellness Advocate for dōTERRA essential oils. She is passionate about sharing the life-enhancing benefits of therapeutic-grade essential oils with the world.

Charlotte is a fully-qualified drama and theatre studies secondary school teacher, a trained Tapping practitioner, a Reiki Master, certified aromaTOUCH therapist and is currently training to become a certified Jack Canfield Train the Trainer.

Charlotte is enthusiastic about helping to inspire and empower mothers through life tools she calls *Butterflies*. Charlotte is also on a mission to educate children to live with passion and purpose, through the medium of original and empowering songs – a project she calls *Kaleidoscope Kids.*

Charlotte trained in Musical Theatre at the Guildford School of Acting – one of the most highly regarded theatre schools in the UK. Charlotte has performed all over the world in some of the most prestigious venues, including Broadway's City Center Theatre (the production, *Pendragon*, won the accolade of the *New York Times* Critics' Choice), The Royal Albert Hall, St. James's Palace and Sir Andrew Lloyd Webber's private Sydmonton home.

Charlotte has also rubbed shoulders with Royalty during her career and appeared in an ITV documentary, *Opening Shots*, featuring Prince Edward. Performing at Sir Andrew Lloyd Webber's televised birthday celebration concert with the National Youth Music Theatre, Charlotte was delighted to work alongside Glenn Close and Antonio Banderas. And for some fun trivia, Charlotte appeared on Channel 4's *Come Dine With Me*. She wowed fellow contestants with her unique culinary delights and won!

Charlotte has a First Class Master's Degree in Creative Writing from Bath Spa University College. She was chosen for the Bath Spa Writers' Anthology with a short story, *Perhaps I Was An Angel.*

Since graduating from Bath Spa, Charlotte, along with her brother, James

KG Benz, co-created and starred in the award-winning black comedy musical, *Creena DeFoouie*. It received rave reviews in London's West End, the International Edinburgh Festival, Canada (winning the Fan Favourite Award) and Off-Broadway's oldest venue, The Cherry Lane Theatre. *Creena DeFoouie* was also selected for the BBC's *Northern Exposures*. Charlotte and her brother have since co-created a dazzling musical, *Rainbow Grace*, for children of all ages. Its debut was in Westport Theatre in the west of Ireland and it has since been performed in the U.K. It has been critically acclaimed.

CHAPTER 14

OVERCOMING DOMAIN REJECTION

BY HOSIAH TAGARA

It is very possible to bring forth your expertise and be resisted in dramatic ways – such that if you do not have an internal conviction you could walk away.

REJECTION

Rejection can leave you with a residue of a sense of unworthiness. If people are going to pay you for who you are and what you have to offer, know that it has to be a factor of the value that you project out of yourself. That's why it is imperative for you to overcome any sense of unworthiness. Actually, that feeling will repel value out of your life. The root of that sense, in many cases and lives, is rejection.

DEALING WITH DOMAIN REJECTION

Rejection is registered when one approaches a person, people, a domain or an opportunity with a hopeful expectation of acceptance, collaborative interaction and optimism only to hit a wall. It means to be deemed wrong or inappropriate. Normally, when this happens, many people suffer internal scars, wounds and sustain significant injuries of the heart – the effect of which can never be underestimated.

Just as a physical accident leaves marks and wounds on the body, circumstances of this nature are scarring. For the body and the soul have one thing, if not two, in common – both of them are part of a human being and both of them feel pain.

Practical situations of rejection include marital complications, professional regrets, failed business ventures, hatred by loved ones, betrayal by friends, refusal of responsibility by parents in childhood and many more. Worse still, when this happens in infancy, the personality, self-belief and self-concept of a person is greatly disabled. This then makes it critical for many people to understand the anatomy of rejection and what gives it its sting, then one can decide how to deal with it.

Can you believe it that Jack Ma, the richest man in China, the 18th richest man in the world and the owner of Alibaba applied for 30 jobs and was rejected for all of them? When KFC entered China, 24 people applied. 23 were taken and he was rejected. He applied at Harvard and was rejected 10 times. Five people, himself included, applied to the police and the other four were accepted and he was not. Yet, now he is estimated to have a fortune worth US$29.7 billion and counting. When you overcome domain rejection, you break forth into favour.

DISMANTLING THE FOUNDATIONS OF REJECTION

Rejection is based on two fundamental concepts – the concept of your **real value** and the concept of your **perceived value**. Your "real value" is the true essence of your being and life, the total summation of your potential, giftedness, talents and graces as packaged in you by the Creator, before you were even formed in your mother's womb. This is 'the real you' as known and made by the Maker.

On the other hand, your "perceived value" is how people, including yourself, view you. It is a subjective value system that people attach to a life when they look at a person. It has a lot to do with the external physical attributes and material assets of a person: looks, skin colour, texture of skin, body structure, the car one is driving, where they met you and so on. This varies in its scale depending on their ability to see beyond the surface.

Having understood the concepts, you will learn that when a person's perceived value of you is less than your real value, they can reject you.

Perceived Value < Real Value => Rejection

But take note of the fact and the truth that this does not mean your life does not have value, but just that people haven't gotten a revelation or understanding of who you are and what you are capable of doing. So, when people have not been privileged to have a revelation of your essence, meaning, value and significance, they can reject you – not because your life doesn't have value, but because they are blinded to it.

On the other hand, when your essence, value, meaning and significance (which is your real value) goes beyond people's perceived value of you, you become intimidating and people can also reject you.

Perceived Value >Real Value => Rejection (Intimidation)

Yet still, take note of the truth and the fact that clearly this does not mean that your life is meaningless or valueless, but intimidating. Between these two extreme scenarios is the specificity of your cause. Otherwise, the truth has nothing to do with your life not having real value, but instead what and how people view you. For God does not make scrap or rejects.

WHY DO PEOPLE MISUNDERSTAND YOU?

First, remember that the reason you do not understand how your car or television works (provided you are not a mechanic or a technician), is because you were not there when they created them, nor did you get educated on their composition, regardless of the fact that you want to use them. Similarly, the fact that others need you and you are valuable to them does not negate the fact that they were not there when your maker loaded you with purpose. They might be part of your reason for existence, but definitely not all of it. Unfortunately, many read or look in the wrong places to get information on your full potential and proper use. In any case:

- You are as mysterious as the Creator in whose image you were created.
- The world and people outside you do not have the capacity to perceive who you really are.
- They are intimidated by you.
- They are blinded to the richness hidden inside of you.

No one puts what is available in the open. You are a concealed revelation wrapped up in time.

WHO LOSES?

Having known how valuable your life is and that rejection has nothing to do with you being insignificant are but blind eyes seeking to describe you. You have to know that whoever rejects you for any reason has lost a lifetime opportunity to be impacted by the value and essence in your life. You have not lost in any way, even if it was an opportunity that you thought you could benefit from. Know that doors don't have value in themselves, but they merely reflect the value of those who enter through them. It is the same with places and positions. Whatever refuses to open for you deprives itself of value. Whoever loves you is honoured and privileged.

If you think you lost when you were rejected, change your attitude and mind-set right away. Know that there is no one who could have touched and impacted their lives the way you could have. Even though it seems as though someone took your place, they could only be themselves, but never you. It's a loss they can never regain. Instead of losing, the truth is, you were preserved. You were made available for what life is coming forward to offer you. "Rejection is a blessing in disguise. It snatches you from being committed to what could be less than the best for you – not because you are not valuable, but to make you available for what life is bringing next."

There are opportunities that are less than one's real value that run ahead of the worthwhile ones in life. They can catch up with us in our blindness. Out of our impatience and ignorance we can jump ahead onto these. When God really wants the best for us as He always does, He will allow the employment of rejection. This is not because you are not valuable, but because you are supposed to be available for what reflects your real value. The real and the genuine are not under pressure because it's real value. The fake has to be first and forge ahead because it can't stand up to compete with the genuine.

Here are a few interesting thoughts:

- A person can be rejected yesterday or today but accepted in the future.
- The same person can be rejected by one but accepted by someone else.
- There is a link between discernment of value and rejection.
- It is rare for one to attach value onto someone they do not accept.
- If people reject you, they will seek to justify it by discounting your value.

I heard it before. I now have known it to be true. One man's meat is another man's poison. Inversely, one man's poison is another man's meat. More interesting than this is the fact that another man's trash is one of God's jewels.

THE REAL YOU

The real you is constituted by what people know about you (the known you) and what people have not known as yet about you (the unknown you). It is the summation of the revealed you and the unrevealed you. It is the aggregate of your past, your present and your future.

Real Value = Known Value + Unknown Value

or

Real You = Revealed You + Unrevealed You

or

Real value = Past + Present + Future

As I established before, your perceived value is how people and you perceive yourself.

Perceived Value = Revealed You = Known You = Past + Present

In most cases, whenever people reject you, it is not on the basis of your real value but on your perceived value. That is, they look at what they know about you, what they were told, what you achieved, what you have done. They rely on your past and your present. The result is what they use to ascertain your acceptability. If the accumulation of all their scores in this category is lower that what they think is right, you can be a prospective candidate for rejection.

Yet the manifestation of the real you might be skewed into your future, which they do not know about. That is the reason why before anyone forms a conclusion about you they need to get a revelation of what the future holds for you.

Having said so, you will learn that even if people reject you on these grounds, if you know who you are, you are able to move on regardless of how they treated you.

GOD CONFIDENCE VERSUS SELF-CONFIDENCE

Out of the revelation of who you really are and how valuable you are, is supposed to be born confidence. Purpose-powered people are characterized by an unshakable confidence about themselves and a visible boldness towards assignment. The degree of your confidence decides the fluidity and the velocity of the flow of potential and grace in your life.

Now, people with a clear revelation of their real value reflect confidence born out of a self-belief that starts and ends with them. This is what I call self-confidence. It's an assurance of acceptance and success that is born out of one's abilities and experience. Unfortunately, such a confidence goes 'face flat' in the event of failure. On the other hand, God-confidence is born out of a revelation of the expertise of the Maker and our trust in his assignment of a mandate to us. Knowing that He has the power and is able and willing to make it available to us as we engage in purpose to do His will, God-confidence has its seat in the unfailing nature of the Creator. Self-confidence stems out of self without any relational trust in the Creator.

It is then out of here that divine influence is born. Confidence is influential. That is why all influential people have it. If a person has self-confidence, such a one will influence like a man can. Now, there is no way one can reflect the confidence of God and not experience the influence of a God kind and size. That is exactly what you need if you are pushing the agenda of the Creator on the earth—God-sized influence.

About Hosiah

Hosiah Tagara is a catalyst of "becoming" and a transformation expert. He is the Founder of WealthMasters Global. A marketplace initiative that is igniting the spirit of Marketplace Dominion through market skilling, opportunity listing and investment mobilization in and for Africa. A business man and an economist by professional training, Hosiah Tagara is a business and life coach to many WealthMasters, government leaders and captains of industry. His insight, ideas, models, templates and wisdom in problem-solving has given him audience and engagement with key leaders in the continent of Africa including Heads of State. He is also the founder of HTI Consultancy Inc. He is also a Co-founder of TexAlytics Inc, a specialized Business Intelligence (BI) outfit offering high value strategic advisory services to businesses and public entities for profitable growth.

Hosiah is a published author of several books including, *The Purpose Powered People, The Dominion Masters* and *Built On The Rock* among many other titles. He is a principal author and contributor to the world's first ever Marketplace Bible. He is a highly sought-after international conference speaker who has travelled to over twenty countries across America, Africa, Asia and Europe. He is a member of the NATIONAL ASSOCIATION OF EXPERTS, WRITERS AND SPEAKERS in the USA. He is the founder of Beam Of Hope Churches International, a network of churches with branches in Zimbabwe, Zambia, South Africa and Canada. His passion is to help people, organizations and communities by becoming the fullness of who they are supposed to be – through value creation and maximizing capacity.

Hosiah Tagara is married to Premadonah Tagara and they are blessed with two children, Tehillah Grace and Eminent Hosiah, Jnr.

You can connect with Hosiah Tagara at:

- hosiah@wealthmasters.co
- www.twitter.com/HosiahTagara
- www.facebook.com/hosiaht
- www.hosiahtagara.com
- www.wealthmasters.co

CHAPTER 15

HOW DISCIPLINE AND HABIT CAN FUEL YOUR SUCCESS!

BY STEVE McNICHOLAS

We are what we repeatedly do.
Excellence then is not an act, it's a habit.
~ Aristotle

In a book entitled Recipe for Success, I am expecting that in every chapter, you are finding numerous 'ingredients' (ideas, concepts, tips and suggestions) that will help deliver the success, achievement and fulfilment you clearly want, and so you should. I have spent almost two decades myself developing my own interest and passion in this field, reading countless books, attending many events and seminars and applying the lessons and principles of many top speakers and teachers in this field.

Time and time again, I see a common pattern, a recipe or a 'code' becoming evident in achieving success. I don't have time in this chapter to explain in detail how to 'unlock the code', it's the subject of my next book, but what I would like you to consider today is a significant foundation in all personal success and achievement, the power of 'habit'. To be more precise, the application of discipline, overcoming the 'easy-ness conundrum' and then critically, embedding the habits you form to move you quickly towards your goals.

There has been plenty of research done of how 'habit' has an enormous influence on your life and several good books of late have been written on the subject. For example, did you know that about half of the decisions you think you make each day are actually habitual. You are not really deciding at all. Your brain is automatically programmed with the habit, so is effectively making that decision for you. You don't 'really' decide to brush your teeth every morning, or check your mobile phone for updates before breakfast, or put your seatbelt on when driving. They are habits you have formed. You probably have several more that you do 'automatically', I know I have. So, when you can apply the formula of positive habit to those areas of your life where you need to, you will be amazed at what you can achieve in such a short period of time – without even thinking too much about it!

I believe we all have hopes, dreams and goals to push for – if you don't, then you are probably not the type of person who would be reading a book such as this. Such hopes and goals usually fall under some familiar themes such as health and fitness, or wealth and finances, or family and relationships or career plans. Often it is a combination of all of them.

Most of the time, we have a pretty good sense of what these goals would actually mean to us, we can picture and describe them and even sense how they might 'feel'. Examples could be describing the way we want our body to look, or the dream job we want to secure and what that would mean in lifestyle, or the change in relationship we want to have with our family and loved ones. We can describe them in detail in our minds, and they give us a sense of what life could be like if...BOOM...reality comes crashing down. Your brain suddenly realises the sheer scale of change being considered here, and the 'noise' kicks in: "don't bother, ...not worth it, ...not got time, ...not going to happen,

…not for you, …way too big" and more often than not, it wins.

Even if you somehow over-rule the noise and you got so inspired by a magazine, for example, to try and build an amazing body, losing 20, 30 or 40 pounds in weight to get there, but after one session at the gym, you ache so much you take a week off and never start again! You finally get the urge to start the novel you have always dreamed about writing and start writing like crazy over the weekend. Once you get back to work and the emails and meetings and other demands kick in, you 'put it off' for a few days then never come back to it. You feel motivated to go in search of a whole different career path in a field you are passionate about, but after researching all the work necessary to achieve this and the uncertainty of change, you are overwhelmed by the task and typically stay doing what you have always done. Sound familiar?

What's happening is that the motivations that created these dreams and goals are also combining to create a type of internal 'frenzy'. It's a place in our minds where we see and feel this goal in great detail. We feel energised to achieve this vision, then suddenly we realise it's too big, too much and it often, despite our best intentions to make a go of it, overwhelms us.

The strategy therefore is in understanding the simple, repeatable disciplines and then habits that, when applied often, can deliver transformational change in whatever aspects of your life you desire. I know it's much more 'sexy and inspiring' to make dramatic proclamations of your path to millionaire status in a year or less, but the big goals you seek are usually somewhat different from the smaller, repeatable disciplines and habits that will get you there.

The good news is that these small crucial disciplines are often 'easy' to do and therefore easy to form into habits. Once you form a habit, like brushing teeth or wearing a seatbelt, it'll happen every time and will push you to amazing success! It's the compounding effect of doing the same positive task day-in-day-out, that has the incredible effect I'm describing here. As the great Jim Rohn once said, "Discipline and habit are the bridge between your goals and actually accomplishing them."

As you apply this thinking in your approach to goal achievement, you will then be introduced to what I call the 'easy-ness conundrum'. Very simply, you will find that taking a big, audacious goal and breaking it down into manageable 'disciplines', will present you with lots of choices, often daily. The task that forces the choice is typically easy to do, and most frustratingly, it's also easy not to do. That's the conundrum!

Let me try and bring this together in a real example. I have a friend, John, who has had a massive, transformational goal for several years to start his own business. He is passionate about personal training and has wanted to do this for a number of years, but he is in a secure, well-paid sales role and is married with two young boys and obvious financial commitments to keep. The goal, the wish, the desire was clear. John could describe it in great detail…a thriving business, his own gymnasium, several trainers hired, lots of happy clients and just as important, having control over his schedule so that he could be with his family at the end of each day when the boys returned from school, something not always possible in his corporate role.

This vision was crystal clear but through our coaching, we finally got to the reasons why such a compelling goal was not happening. 'We have not saved enough money yet. I have not found the right premises or finances yet. I will stay here for another year to try and earn bonus. I can't hire anyone until I'm booked up myself. I can't go big on social media and marketing yet in case my boss finds out!' Frankly and bluntly, I told him it was never going to happen while he focused so much on the sheer scale of the goal. The happiness and fulfilment he knew this goal would provide him and his family was being swallowed up by the fears, worries, doubts and challenges of what the goal represented.

So, over a period of a month, we broke the goal down into small component disciplines. We took one HUGE goal and broke it into eight different tasks essential to make this happen—tasks that would soon become habits.

Activities that by themselves were relatively 'easy' to do. Examples included:

- Thirty minutes every lunchtime researching the websites and services of local gyms and personal trainers. Instead of wasting time trawling his social media as he would typically do over lunch, he formed a daily discipline to know his market, know his competition, look for the websites he liked and lifted and shifted those ideas to help design his own.

- One hour every evening when the boys were in bed, he began researching property sites for possible locations. He read up on commercial finance options. He developed email contact with local agents who could tell him when leases were up for renewal on potential sites. He got to know the market and instead of watching irrelevant TV every evening, he became obsessed with the task. In two months, he was an expert on the local health and fitness market and all the possible options for financing a new business.

- In order to build confidence and hone his training skills, he offered to run a free exercise class every Friday in the company seminar room for staff. The employer was happy as it kept staff in the office later on Fridays! Within 5 weeks, he had a full class of 24 colleagues all enjoying his free, high octane, motivating training sessions. In two months, he was running two classes, both full and with a waiting list! In effect, he had already found his first fifty potential clients without a penny spent yet on external marketing and confirmation that his training methods and routines were popular!

Now there was a bit more to our plan than just the above examples, but I want to highlight the power here of discipline and the 'easy-ness conundrum' that helped form the habits. Think about the three examples above. None of them in themselves you would call impossible, or even that difficult. In fact, I would say each task was 'easy' to do. Spending 30 minutes of his lunch on researching the market is easy for John to do but so is spending time aimlessly scrolling his social media feeds for crap! He did it every lunchtime for several weeks. Just 30 minutes each day. It became a habit after two weeks. It would have been easy when the kids were in bed after a long day at work to just put TV on and chill until bed.

In itself, logging on the laptop and researching commercial property and finance is not that difficult so he spent an hour every evening. It became obsessional in a good way. It became a positive habit and he just did it without having to think about it. Same with the free classes, easy to cancel them and go home on a Friday after a long week, but just as easy to run them, feel the energy and build up his prospective future client base!

His big, huge goal was forming and taking shape quickly, successfully and through a number of smaller, repeatable disciplines that he found easy to do. That's the 'easy-ness' conundrum, what choices do you make in progressing to your goals?

I am delighted to say that John left his corporate role and founded his own training and fitness business some two years ago as I write this chapter. I am even more pleased to say the business is thriving and he has just hired his tenth employee. His first twenty-five paying clients were former colleagues who attended his free Friday classes!

Now your goals or dreams may not be as big as launching a business or they may be even bigger than that, but whatever they are, consider the three lessons from the above:

1. Don't stop setting goals! Set goals that inspire you and give you purpose but break down the big, huge inspiring goal into several smaller disciplines and focus your attention on building repetition here.

2. Make those disciplines a regular, scheduled occurrence that you will commit to and make them 'easy' to do. Set a time slot daily and do not compromise on it.

3. When faced with the choice of 'easy to' and 'easy not to', which you will face countless times, push on, lean in and take action. After a week or two, it will become habit and you won't even have to think about it after that as you progress positively to the big, huge, inspiring goal!

Let me close by wishing you every success, may the Recipe for Success push you to amazing fulfilment and achievement and you will be inspired to win in life.

About Steve

Steve McNicholas has spent some twenty years developing his research, knowledge and passion for personal development, achievement and helping people succeed. His personal mission statement which he has had for many years is simply 'to inform, inspire and maximise the potential in all people – unlocking the code to help develop winners in life and business'.

After a highly successful career in corporate life, he has recently gone on to launch his own business in speaking, training and coaching clients to 'unlock the code' both in a personal development sense and also in the commercial environment helping clients in the corporate world. Steve does this through his own seven-step approach, having identified those critical stages or 'source codes' underpinning personal success and achievement. He is enjoying great success and is now after much demand, turning his seven step methodology into his latest book, *Unlock the Code: 7 Steps To Your Success*. The book is due for release in early 2019.

With a successful corporate career across a number of industries (telecom, banking, business services), and in holding several executive positions over the past twenty-five years, Steve has developed a reputation with his clients as a 'practioner' and not a guru! He has the bumps, scars and bruises of leading many teams and individuals to amazing levels of success and achievement over the years. It is through this experience, and his own considerable time in researching and developing his thinking and theories here, that he has been able to hone his methodology to the proprietary seven-step process referred to. Steve is therefore able to to appreciate and understand the many challenges that following such a path demands, and that the 'doing' is equally as important as the 'learning'.

Steve is an accomplished keynote speaker and presenter and is comfortable in presenting his material and thinking in small groups as well as in audiences of several hundred. He is a personal coach to several clients and also delivers his material via group workshops designed to help all attendees 'unlock the code' to their success.

You can contact Steve via:

- Website: http://www.stevemcnicholas.com
- LinkedIn: www.linkedin.com/in/steve-mcnicholas-46a38321/
- Facebook: www.facebook.com/steve.mcnicholas.560
- Twitter: @SteveMcUTC

CHAPTER 16

SUCCESS FROM THE NINE C'S OF SELF

BY RICHARD HARRY JOHNSON

I sat in the waiting room of the eye hospital for the sixth time, at what was probably the lowest point in my life. Not only had they found something at the back of one of my eyes, but my sight was diminished in both eyes. I was told it was a clear sign that my retinas were going to detach and all I could do was wait for it to happen. As if that wasn't enough, I had a worryingly large number of ulcers on my esophagus and throat, and a mouth full of them. An oncologist was assigned who sent me for MRI scans to see if there was anything more sinister lurking.

I had lost so much weight, my hair was falling out, I couldn't see properly, and my voice was all but gone. How could this be? I was a health practitioner, treating myself as I would my clients, supplementing, meditating, eating well, trying to keep as fit as possible, but I realized for the first time, I no longer had a handle on my health.

This was until my business partner Christian said to me that I should work with my 'Parts'. I knew of 'parts work' but had assumed this was for trauma. I had no trauma. Or so I thought. I had nothing to lose so I tentatively booked in to see our resident

177

clinical psychotherapist Charmain, and started the Evidence-Based Psychotherapy modality, Internal Family Systems Therapy founded by Richard Schwartz.

On my third session, I had the most profound 'release' of old stories locking me into the past and producing all the symptoms I was experiencing. Within two weeks, miraculously, every one of my symptoms had gone. Completely gone. Another couple of trips to the baffled oncologist and eye hospital both confirmed that everything had cleared. I write this story two years later; none of the symptoms have returned and I still feel the extraordinary benefits of the most life-changing process that I experienced earlier.

Even though I have always been a huge believer in the Mind-Body link to health and disease, this was my personal next level of understanding.

What I discovered is that at the heart of who we really are, is a powerful life force. In this model I refer to this as 'Self'. From here we feel the following qualities innate within us:

1. **Compassion**
2. **Curiosity**
3. **Calm**
4. **Creativity**
5. **Connectedness**
6. **Confidence**
7. **Courage**
8. **Clarity**
9. **Comedy**

The exciting prospect is that you can reinstall this operating system, and with practice and healing it will lead you away from all those innate expressions of who you are.

The emotions that aren't expressed by Self, anger, resentment, grief, hatred, frustration, disdain, confusion, envy and sabotage are all expressions of your Internal Family system. These individual voices form a network of navigation and supply your unconscious thoughts second by second, delivering you with all the formulas and thoughts and incentives to keep you operating from your 'fight, flight or freeze' response – aka: your comfort zone.

From this understanding, I am now learning to operate from this place of Self. The more led by Self I become, I'm noticing astonishing results and upgrades in the evolution of my business.

Here are some suggestions as to how you can find these qualities in your work to propel you forward:

1. <u>Compassion</u>

For me, compassion is key. It is what makes us human, and having compassion for everyone helps us create a peaceful world. My staff commit to devoting their working week to assist me in the driving forward of my businesses. I am so passionate about the public having access to my products and my team; they are paramount to this venture. It takes nothing for me to be understanding when they have a break-up in a relationship, or a ceiling fall in at home, or a fall out with a family member. If I provide a service within my team to assist them through a life challenge, the burden of that life challenge doesn't grow into a mountain and doesn't leave them in need of time off from work with stress or sickness.

My team members are my family, and they work very hard to assist me with my vision. Bringing compassion into your place of work lifts the lid off it becoming the daily grind. I remember my first job being in that trap. That existence of a life is one I would never wish on an employee. I try my best to provide them with the necessary services to help them through their personal life. If you work alone, remember to show yourself some compassion in just the same way.

2. Curiosity

When a member of staff comes up with an idea, we can be all too quick to detail how five years ago it didn't work. Instead sit with curiosity and ask them the all-important:

- WHY?
- WHAT?
- WHO?
- WHEN?
- HOW?

Your member of staff might have the vital missing link that you would never have discovered if you would have simply told them that it won't work.

Also keep curious when a customer doesn't appreciate one of your products. It is easy to dismiss negative feedback with the assumption that. . .'We can't please everyone'. This blanket statement can really stop you going into the fearful place of questioning your products. When I ask our customers for feedback, I explain that it's nice to receive the good reviews, but it's the constructive criticism that keeps me striving to improve. If a customer feels I have failed in some way, I remain curious and see what I can uncover. If you slam your customer for not liking you, you've missed the lesson. Stay curious and look for the important message they are trying to show you.

If you have a new idea, be curious and try it out. Replace fear of the unknown with curiosity, as curiosity is the spark behind the spark of every great idea.

3. Calm

This mind of yours of can run the equivalent of 10 marathons a day. How exhausting! The breath is your lifeforce, if you let your body breathe all day without consciously navigating it, you will become locked in all your usual behavioral patterns and thoughts. Find space in the day for taking seven long breaths and inviting calm to initiate in your system. Try doing this after every hour of work. The breathing can really activate you and change your state. If you give it your attention and take charge of it, you will feel the rewards almost instantly.

4. Creativity

So many people say, "I don't have a creative bone in my body". False. Try to stop your cells creating scar tissue when you cut yourself. Try to stop your senses enjoying tasting good food. Ask your body not to enjoy your favorite piece of music. Tell your eyes not to trigger bliss in your body when you see an island that looks like paradise. You are creativity. It is at the core of who you are.

There is a creative solution to all the challenges you will ever face in business. But how are you or your team connecting to creativity? You and your team deserve to play. At 48 years of age, I began singing lessons. Through singing, I felt transformed and open, ideas flowed and shyness lifted. Wonderful shifts happen when you follow your creativity and do something that may challenge you.

5. Connectedness

Which part of your business do you outsource to another company? Maybe your business cards are printed by a local business. Your window cleaner works for you. Your accountancy firm does your end-of-year books. There is a network of businesses all around you ready and willing to assist with their expertise. Build a relationship with these people. They know more people than you may have considered. You need their products, but have you considered they might have networks that you are not yet plugged into? It just starts with a conversation.

Don't just build your own community, plug into the existing ones out there. Your hairdresser will talk to several clients about your exciting new plans. The newsagent will know the very person you are looking for to upgrade your new website. The internet also holds amazing networks of potential online communities. Roger Hamilton's visionary GeniusU is outstanding. We need to connect more and more with community and community is growing exponentially.

6. Confidence

Confidence relates to purpose. What is your purpose in life and does your business and your product embody this purpose? One of the businesses I have that is now in its 18th year is a school-teaching remedial bodywork. I know that at any hour of the working week, I could guess approximately 1,000 members of the public are getting their injuries or pain worked on by my graduates, all over the world. The purpose of this business is to be a part of the infrastructure that can assist the public in getting out of pain. Don't be afraid to be so 'bold' as to feel good about your purpose or your bigger vision of your work. When you deliver from your purpose, your confidence in your work is grounded. Be authentic, and your authenticity will shine through. Add confidence to this and you will be unstoppable.

7. Courage

Courage is the ability to leverage everything you know on a spark of inspiration. Imagine a sling shot. You must really pull that elastic as far back as you can if you really want to propel your vision forward fearlessly to see how far it can go. Testing the waters by only gently pulling the elastic will see that vision land right at your feet. Aiming at a target for how far you want to go may sometimes be necessary, but can also put limits on how far you could really go if you took away any preconceptions. When you really know you are onto something, draw back that sling as far as you possibly can. The only limit to its success is your courage.

8. Clarity

The more you lead your business from a place of Self the more clarity there is. This is the magic of Self leadership, you can see through a new lens of the present, but your internal system sends you into the past and can fearfully conduct your business. The past always informs the future and will always deliver you what you fear. Clarity is a product of conscious Self-led choices. Be in the present and connect to any of the qualities above for guidance with your internal questioning.

9. Comedy

No matter how painful a situation has been in your life, time is a healer. Smile at the tricky situations of the past and know on some level that you were meant to be taught lessons from them. Whenever you are activated by stress, find some calm and see if you can find that inner smile. You will always grow from all the lessons you get. But you can start to pave out a new future where you can learn lessons proactively, as opposed to getting the lessons through being defeated by life events.

I believe the nine C's of Self are a powerful lesson for us all. Type out the words and put them up in your office or study. Get embodying them more and more and watch how, when you are operating more consciously through being Self-led, the magic, luck and enjoyment you are seeking starts to come out to play.

If you would have told me two years ago I could I sit and type these words with perfectly good eyesight, my fears would have told you otherwise. Even the fact that I have had the opportunity to contribute to this amazing book is testament to the fact that this system of operating is so powerful that it can open new and exciting challenges and possibilities.

I hope that my experience instills in you a new way of looking at things to bring about positive changes in your life and business.

About Richard

Richard Harry Johnson helps his clients obtain success through Coaching, Education and Health.

With almost 30 years' experience in the health and wellbeing field, Richard has worked successfully with thousands of happy clients, organisations and businesses, and continues to combine his coaching practice with writing and developing new training courses in health, wellbeing, personal development and enterprise.

In 1999, Richard founded the Sports Therapy Organisation – which has gone on to become the UK's largest Professional Association for sports injury professionals, and has well-established international links. This was followed in 2000 by the founding of Active Health Group, which has established itself as the leading global provider of Sports Therapy training and Integrative Health Practitioner training.

Richard's philanthropic tendencies were realised with the founding of the Sports Therapy Foundation, which as well as providing educational grants and bursaries, has built and funds the 'Active Health Malawi' clinic, which provides free musculoskeletal treatments in Mulanje, Malawi. (This is sadly one of the poorest countries in the world, with virtually no access to healthcare, and no welfare system.)

In 2016, Richard realised through his own health concerns that most of the healthcare systems in place were very disjointed. Through this he set about using his entrepreneurial talents to create a whole new health industry, and the Integrative Health Society was born. This Society aims to bring together health practitioners across the globe who recognise the need to treat the mind, body and spirit holistically for the best outcomes.

As a keen advocate of education, Richard understands the needs of easily accessible training, and launched the very popular AHG Online Academy. He is also keen on his own ongoing education and commits to a minimum of eight weeks of continuing professional development each year and to achieve his PhD by age 55. He also appreciates the need for Professional Associations, to not only provide support to their members and industry, but also as an acknowledgement of one's qualifications and skills.

With this in mind, as well as being the Founder Member of both the Sports Therapy Organisation and the Integrative Health Society, Richard is a member of many leading prestigious associations, including the British Association of Sport & Exercise Medicine, the International Federation of Sports Medicine, the Royal Society of Medicine, the Institute of Noetic Sciences, the American Board of NLP & Hypnotherapy, the Association for Coaching, the UK Association of Health Coaches, The Nutrition Society and the Complementary & Natural Healthcare Council, amongst others.

It is through these associations that Richard keeps up-to-date with all the latest research and news on a wide range of health professions. To keep current in the world of business and enterprise, Richard is also a member of the Institute of Directors and the Institute of Training and Occupational Learning.   Richard is also part of the Entrepreneurs Institute, GeniusU programme.

When not working or studying, Richard's passions are animals and animal welfare, singing, esotericism, and personal development.

You can connect with Richard at:

- www.richardharryjohnson.com
- www.twitter.com/richhjohnson01
- www.facebook.com/richardharryjohnson

CHAPTER 17

THREE BEDROCK PRINCIPLES FOR CREATING A LIFE, NOT JUST A LIVING

BY PAULA BLACK

Insights to help you grow your business or career without sacrificing your personal life and happiness.

I have been a business development speaker and coach to lawyers, entrepreneurs, and professionals for many, many years. Along the way, I've observed the many challenges, obstacles, and myths they face as they pursue advancement in their careers, grow their businesses, and try to fit it all into their lives. Here are three of the bedrock principles I discovered that help lawyers, entrepreneurs, and professionals advance in their businesses without sacrificing their personal lives.

1. **Tailor your work to fit in harmony with your life. And don't waste one minute feeling inadequate. No one gets to define your work-life balance but you.**

   Work-life balance? Who came up with that phrase *work-life*

balance anyway? I would like to inform them that we only have one life to live. *Our life is our work and our family and our friends and our hobbies and our errands, etc., etc., etc.* It's all one life, and we need to integrate it all, and not to feel guilty about whatever it is we are doing or not doing.

The reality is, work-life balance does not exist. If by chance everything aligns and you achieve it, it's only for a fleeting moment; it's not sustainable. So what if we looked at it from a different perspective? What is sustainable is to have all parts of your life in harmony. In an orchestra, sometimes the brass section is more dominant and other times it's the strings. The goal is always to be in harmony. You can't compartmentalize your life. You have to look at your life holistically. Your career, your business, your family, your hobbies—its ALL your life.

A lawyer—we'll call her April—loved her work, but prioritized spending time with her 'special needs' child. How can she possibly have it all? April decided to look at what she loves about her work through the lens of what is best for her entire family. She started setting priorities and goals. She loves managing people and thought she would like to be manager of her office—until she realized her child was likely to suffer the consequence of her staying later at the office.

As it was, April was already commuting an hour and a half each way. But then she found a great job opportunity—her dream job—where she could do work she loves. She moved the family to a neighborhood where her new job was located. The three hours she had been spending commuting were now spent with her family. April has achieved harmony in her life. She loves her job and it is now possible to run out to take her child to a doctor's appointment and get back to the office in no time. "What I learned about myself is that I don't stop being a mom at work and I don't stop being a lawyer at home," said April.

How can you pursue harmony in your life like April did? Make these adjustments:

- **Manage expectations.** Make sure your family, friends, and colleagues know what to expect. Don't make promises you can't keep. And when the unexpected happens, communicate the change as soon as possible. At the office, when you need to run out to your child's recital, announce that you have an appointment and when you will be back. As a professional you do not have to report the details of where you are going; it's none of their business. But they do need to know when you will be back and if you will be reachable. And reachable means that you can let a call go to voicemail and you will return the call when you are ready to focus on your work.

- **Get help.** Yes, hire people to do what you can't do, don't want to do, or don't have time to do. Let us not forget, Superman and Wonder Woman are comic book characters and have no place in our real lives. Learn to delegate while retaining control.

- **Learn to say no.** Say no to annoying, unimportant, and useless things that waste your time.

You get to choose the life that works for you. Strive for harmony with all areas of your life.

2. Examine your assumptions. If they don't apply to your life today, rewrite them.

Are you pre-programmed with what you should do, with no room for what you want to do? Is your comfort zone killing you? Has complacency set in? Are you just going through the motions? Is complacency sucking the oxygen out of your dreams, your courage, and your passion?

We have many assumptions about the way things must be done. When we stop to really examine them, we often find they are outdated or weren't valid in the first place. It takes courage to believe in yourself when you have little evidence that you will be successful. It takes wisdom to apply the skills you honed in a different way or another environment.

Whether you are looking to build your practice where you are, find a new job, start your own company, or just stop the madness, you can make it happen!

My client—we'll call her Elizabeth—is a private banker who, after fifteen years, found herself no longer happy at a prestigious national bank. Elizabeth assumed she would retire from there, so thought she just had to endure the situation. "I was on cruise control and doing exactly what I thought I should be doing. I liked my clients and the money was good. For reasons that were perplexing to me, the more I succeeded, the more miserable I felt. My management made me feel that I was never enough, even though I was the top producer in the region for a long, long time," said Elizabeth.

Worse still, Elizabeth realized that the added time she was spending trying to resolve her problems at work was taking her away from her true priorities: her family, animals, and helping her private banking clients.

So it was time for Elizabeth to examine her assumptions. Did she really want to endure her situation until retirement? She had a choice. She went on five interviews, found that her skills and experience were highly marketable, and received two job offers with substantial increases in income. She was looking for a more suitable environment, not money, but that was a nice byproduct.

Sometimes when you have been with the same organization for years and years, you have no perception of your true value. You can only see your value through the lens of one organization.

I invite you to ask yourself: Is this what I really want to do with my life? Here are four tips to help you see things differently and make progress as Elizabeth did:

- **Challenge your beliefs.** I don't know enough. I'm not smart enough. They won't hire me. I can't do that. These are all lies we tell ourselves so we don't have to commit to something. It's safe. But nothing worthwhile ever grew from taking the safe path.

- **Take every chance to hone your skills.** Be ready when opportunity knocks. Who knows, opportunity just might emerge from your newfound skills.

- **Rejection doesn't mean you should stop what you're doing.** Learn from it and find another way to proceed. And do that again and again and again.

- **Take a chance.** Does your thirteen-year-old self still have dreams that speak to you?

Maybe it's time for you to take a good, long look at your situation. Take inventory of what you like and what is troubling you. If you can be honest, you will see the situation clearly and you can start crafting a strategy to move forward to a better life.

3. **Make a commitment! It's the essential ingredient that will move mountains. Without commitment there is little progress, only lateral movement that is no better than stagnation.**

Management expert Ken Blanchard once said, "There's a difference between interest and commitment. When you're interested in doing something, you do it only when it's convenient. When you're committed to something, you accept no excuses, only results."

Commitment isn't a matter of willpower. It's what wakes us up in the morning and calls us to action. It drives us to believe we can change the world.

An entrepreneur—we'll call her Samantha—was frustrated with herself because for two years she wanted to write a book, but could never get started. She said she couldn't decide what she should write about, even though she had lots of knowledge and expertise in her field. One day we were talking about the women in her field that she admired. She talked about their strength, their courage, and their vision.

Bingo! Samantha's face lit up; she'd found a book idea she could commit to. She was so excited at the thought of talking to all those women she admired. She started calling them and one after another said she would be honored to be in her book. Samantha explains, "In spite of the fact that I had no relationship with any of these women, they were eager to be in my book. I was blown away by that."

Samantha worked on the details: editing, publishing, and launching. Her commitment paid off, and it came together in three months.

Here are three suggestions to help you figure out what can get you up and into action in the same way that Samantha moved from an interesting idea to an unstoppable commitment:

- **Find your passion and commit to it.** You don't have to know how in order to begin. The path will reveal itself and lead you forward in all sorts of inconceivable ways.

- **Just take the first step.** Do the work. Do the research and listen to your gut. You'll rarely be a hundred percent sure it will work, but you can always be a hundred percent sure that doing nothing won't work.

- **What if things go wrong, you may ask?** But what if things go right, and what if the course of your life is changed in unimaginable ways? Take a chance with unbridled commitment. Meet doubt, complacency, and resistance head on, and don't let them get in the way and hold you back or stop you.

Have you ever had a feeling that vibrates in your gut over and over again? It's telling you there is more to life, or that you don't have to accept your situation, or that there is something better waiting for you. Do you listen? Is it just an interesting thought or is it something worth committing to—a commitment to act? Do you want more? Imagine the possibilities. What have you always had the desire to do, and with whom? Listen to your gut. The reward could be a fulfilling life.

Take the first step. The timing may never look right. In fact, it will always look scary. Trust your gut and commit.

These three bedrock principles shaped the lives and seeded joy and fulfillment for these women. These principles can do the same for you. It's time to take ownership of your future. Tailor your work to fit in harmony with your life; create a life of your own making, a life you want. Examine your assumptions, embrace change with a sense of adventure, and have the courage to make it happen. Make a commitment, let your passion drive you, celebrate progress, and shake off adversity. Live the life you want. Find joy in your work and harmony in your life. And I wish you more fulfillment than you have ever imagined!

About Paula

Paula Black is one of the world's leading business development coaches for lawyers, entrepreneurs and service professionals. She teaches her clients how to attract more clients and grow their businesses while still having the personal life they really want.

Paula was voted one of the Top Legal Business Development Coaches and is a member of the Forbes Coaching Council. Her most gratifying work is one-on-one coaching where she can witness the growth and change that individual's experience with her guidance.

Here is what a few clients have to say about the experience.

"Paula makes me look at the hard decisions and see that there is another way, even when I am blocked. Sometimes I am too close to a situation and she gives me a different perspective.

She once spent an entire Sunday with me to develop my business plan when I wanted to propose partnership to my now partner. I felt I was not worthy and after spending the day with her I experienced an 'aha' moment—I was not only worthy, I was going to make this business amazing and successful. That was four years ago and my business is amazing and successful. Paula showed me that I could be the change maker and I had the power—she was right!"

Small business owner, Partner

"The impact Paula has made is by making that voice of reason so loud and ever present that when I am faced with decisions, I now find myself pausing to listen and hear that voice in the back of my head."

Entrepreneur

"Paula provided me with solid, sound practical advice that energized me and helped give me the confidence I needed that the lull in my practice could be overcome (it has!).

I know she is always there if I need her. That, in and of itself, is a confidence builder. Paula is top notch; she's my 'secret sauce."

Litigation practice chair, large regional firm

She is an award-winning and bestselling author of *The Little Black Book* series and has recently published her fifth book, *A Lawyer's Guide to Creating a Life, Not Just a Living.*

She is a business development expert and in the past has consulted on marketing for a wide range of clients including Burger King, Deloitte, Office Depot, The New Times Syndicate and the Jimmy Buffett–Herman Wouk musical, *Don't Stop The Carnival.*

Paula is a frequent keynote speaker and media guest. When she's not creating solutions to solve her clients' biggest issues, you'll find her taking cooking classes from local chefs in places like Tuscany, San Miguel de Allende or Hong Kong.

You can connect with Paula at:

- Paula@PaulaBlack.com
- www.Twitter.com/LegalBranding
- www.Facebook.com/PaulaBlackLegal

CHAPTER 18

CLAIM YOUR DREAM CAREER, EVEN IF...

BY KARINE EINANG

I want to tell you a story, a story about a brown-eyed girl who just turned 16. A girl that is about to go for her big dream: moving abroad for one year, to the land of freedom and opportunities.

One year away from little Norway, to experience the life in the southern part of the US, has been her dream for years. She has studied English, and she has prepared for living away from her family for the next 11 months. She has become best friends with her host family who are so nice and who lets her live with them as a daughter and sister through this school year.

The day before she leaves her hometown and says goodbye to everyone, to start her adventure in a foreign country, she feels that something is not right. A few hours later, her world is turned upside down. She is not critically sick, she is not about to die, even if she feels that her world is suddenly falling apart. She is pregnant...

Her world didn't fall apart, I know – because I was that brown-eyed girl longing for a year in a country far away. And what could have become a disaster, turned out to be a blessing in disguise. I took it step-by-step, joined my local school, and was back in the classroom when my daughter was one week old.

What has all this to do with claiming your dream career? I will tell you in a little while…

You see, even if I got pregnant at the age of 16, my life wasn't over. Of course it wasn't. It brought new opportunities, new experiences. I don't encourage anyone to become a young teenage mom, a child should not have a child… But, when it happens, we have to turn it into something good.

I did. I worked really hard at school so that nobody should say I was a bad mother, or a stupid girl getting pregnant. I trained my mindset on how to find new solutions, how to see the positive when everything seemed so negative. I visualized the good, and the good was what I got. I practiced something I called my even -if-mindset: «even if it is what it is, I will do my best».

Of course, I could have stopped. I could have used all the excuses in the world. But I didn't, because I know we are all here on this earth a short amount of time, and we have to make the best of it…for ourselves and for those around us. I used the even-if-mindset to take the next step. The next step towards the rest of my life…

I transformed my life from being a young girl, wanting to experience the world, to end up as a single mother, still wanting to experience whatever life wanted to show me. And this life showed me a lot. It showed me new careers, from being a secretary to becoming an HR Manager. It showed me happiness and sorrow.

The years went by and I ended up married…and divorced…with two small children. Instead of feeling sorry for myself, I got my «even-if mindset» back on track. (I just love the even-if mindset!)

Long story short: I quit my job as an HR Manager to go back to school. Someone would have explained that with one word: «CRAZY». But I did, even if...

I went all in, and ended up as a fire chief. A job that let me work with people, work with my passion – and a job that was so «me». But after 15 years in the fire department, something happened. I was afraid. Afraid of going to work. Afraid of what was on the other side of my front door when the doorbell rang at home. I became an angry, confused, bitter and totally stressed-out woman. I didn't want to live. All I wanted was to get some rest, and let my family get their life back. I knew that I had been hard on them, the same way I had been hard on myself. I ended up diagnosed with PTSD (post-traumatic stress disorder).

Today, I know that I couldn't see things straight. Today, I know that they wouldn't be better off without me around. My winning card was that I decided to be open about having PTSD. I was open about my fears, my desire to step out of this world. . .and that was what saved my life.

With amazing help from my associates, my family, my friends, and even some people I didn't know, but who had heard what I went through, and by an angel of a psychologist, I got my life back. I'm touched sitting here thinking of how warm-hearted they were to me. They reached out because I had cried for help. I was blessed.

Getting my life back together, I started to feel that I had to do something else, something away from the fire department. I wanted to work with something that could give me energy, something that could give me joy, something that allowed me to help others who were now in a place where I once was. And something that let me travel back and forth from our hometown in Norway, to the southern US.

Oh Yes! I still had the same dream that I had when I was a 16-year-old, brown-eyed girl.

I had promised myself that I should one day experience a life in the southern states, and I intended to stick to that promise!

My vision of having a career that matched my desire was easier said than done. The truth was, I didn't know what to do, or where to start. I didn't know what my mission really was, or how I could manage to pay the bills if it didn't work out.

But I couldn't continue the path I was on. I had to go that extra mile to learn everything I now know about making a thriving career transformation – and I did! I ended up having the key to a successful transformation – and it felt much better than winning the lottery (for me it felt like I was in possession of the winning ticket...).

Now I'm so excited to share the key to a successful career transformation with you. Let me show you with three powerful steps.

Just promise me one thing before I share these steps with you:

DON'T EVER GIVE UP ON YOUR DREAM!

Step 1: Going back to basics - only Better

The first step is all about going back to basics. This is the foundation of your career transformation. By going back to basics, you ask yourself questions. For example:

- Why do you want to change your career?
- What are you passionate about?
- What could you do *even if* you didn't get a dollar doing it?
- What are your fears, and why?
- What are your values, both in your career and in your personal life?
- What will happen if you continue on the path you are on?

Make an effort in answering these questions. And be honest.

Let me explain one of the questions. The question about fear...

Fear is our biggest enemy, and we all know how fear can stop us from doing the right thing... going after what we really want. But fear can also become our best friend...if we do the right things in the right order. Think of fear as a warning sign. It's there to make you focused and awake. It's human to be afraid of the unknown.

Write down ALL the things that you are afraid of regarding transforming your career.

Then you categorize them like this:

1. **The fears you can't influence.**
   – Maybe you write down the fear of someone laughing at you if you fail, or that you're afraid of making a fool of yourself. These fears are out of your control. You can't do anything about them. All you can do is be nice to the people around you, and not be influenced by what other people say or do.
2. **The fears that are not real.**
   – For example: what if I never get a second chance in my life if I don't make it?
3. **The fears that are real.**
   – For example: what if I don't make it, or what if I don't have the skills needed?

This is quite an exercise! How strange it may sound - it's a fun one!

By writing down and getting in touch with your fears, you start seeing that some of them are NOT worth thinking about. You are supposed to draw a big X over *the fears you can't influence* and **the fears that are not real.**

The one category that is left **(the real fears)** is what you are going to be working on. Come up with three different solutions on each of those real fears. Like I said: some of them are good for you to have. They are there to awaken you. Let them become your friends – and a part of your goal! The solution is what you are going to work on next!

The best part with going back to basics is that you are going to dig deep down into how your life can turn out if you have claimed your dream career; if you wake up every morning knowing that you have a job you love, a job that gives you meaning and fulfillment. I think you will sit there smiling as you write down how your life could turn out... Am I right?

Step 2: Plan and Adjust

Something so simple – but yet so frustrating.

You have to plan your transformation, and have focus on the «right» things. Otherwise you end up with everything but results. By planning and adjusting you will learn valuable lessons, like how to find the right resources, and how to take actions that are needed to step out.

What do you have to do in order to claim your dream career? Do you have to go back to school? Do you have to learn some special skills? Or is it your own mind-blocks you have to work on?

Imagine you want to visit a beautiful island in a sailboat. You have to plan for the trip. «Is it something you have to learn before you go? What is a must to bring along? What dangers can you meet?»

You see, if you don't do any planning – you get anything but a safe travel....

Then, let's say you have planned the trip well. As the wind and the waves influence your journey. . . You have to adjust your sails. When you do your planning and adjusting, it will fast track your way to the life and income you deserve and desire.

We love fast tracking, either in business or other areas of our life, right?!

Step 3: Have that coach in your corner

I am the first to admit that getting a coach was not in my mind when I wanted to claim my dream career after turning 40. I thought that it was too expensive or that it would take too long for me to get where I wanted to be. I knew that all the best athletes and CEOs had their coach, but. . .me? I was a woman who «just» wanted to change my career. And hey! I had done it before, right?

If you don't get the help you need you will keep wondering on your own. «Where to start? What to do? How to do it? Am I on the right path?...»

It's just like a hamster wheel. It's not a good feeling.

Find that one person who has been in your shoes, the one you have the right chemistry with. Think of it like someone sitting in the front seat with you, guiding you from A to Z. Find that person who can gain you clarity, and help you take the right steps at the right time, so you can go out there and claim your dream career!

GET YOURSELF THAT «EVEN-IF MINDSET» AND GET GOING!

About Karine

Karine Einang is a career transformation and mindset coach who helps her clients transform their career so that they can wake up every morning and crave for a new day!

Becoming a mother at the age of 16, Karine suddenly had to transform her life, which did something to her. Later on her path, she has had several transformations in her career. From being an HR Manager to becoming a firefighter, and later on a fire chief, is quite a transformation. Then again, she made a huge shift in her career – becoming an entrepreneur and CEO of her own company.

People started asking Karine how she made the leap to her new careers, and how she managed to transform her life the way she had done, becoming a mother at a young age, and then being diagnosed with PTSD (Post Traumatic Stress Disorder) in her late thirties. Karine realized that her experiences, both good and bad, could help others. So she started out guiding people who needed a career transformation, centered around her philosophy—*«Having your dream career – you can live the life you deserve and desire».*

Karine's mission is to guide people through their career transformation so they can live the life they desire. People who want to transform their career have a lot of questions, a lot of fears – and they often don't know WHAT their new career path really is. By asking the right questions, and lovingly guiding her clients towards their desire in life, Karine is «holding her clients' hands» from A to Z.

Like Karine says…
«We have limited time here on earth. We deserve to enjoy life to the fullest while we're around! Our career is an important piece in the puzzle called life, whether we like it or not. When we can't stand our career, it reflects on the rest of our life.

It breaks my heart when someone says that their life seems to pass them by. They freak out at home because of all the stress at work. They work their butt off, trying to stay happy and nice. They are completely fed up, but have no idea what to do with their job and their situation». Because of stories like these, Karine knows she has a mission. Her own story almost cost her the family, and her life...

Karine has a bachelor's degree in Economics and Leadership. She has gone through the Norwegian Fire Academy to become a firefighter and an officer. Later on her path, she became an HSE engineer and a fire engineer. She is also educated in fire investigation and readiness management. In addition, she is a certified NLP Practitioner, and also an assertiveness and life coach.

In 2016, she wrote a Norwegian book about leadership called, *Help! I've become The Boss!* This book is a roadmap for leaders – so they can do their best for the people around and take care of themselves at the same time.

You can connect with Karine at:

- contact@karineeinang.com
- www.karineeinang.com
- www.facebook.com/KarineEinang